SUPER BOWL XXXVIII

32-29

SUPER BOWL XXXIX

24-21

The Boston Globe

This book is available in quantity at special discounts for your group or organization. For further information, contact:
Triumph Books
542 South Dearborn Street, Suite 750
Chicago, Illinois 60605
Phone: (312) 939-3330
Fax: (312) 663-3557

Printed in the United States of America
ISBN-13: 978-1-57243-841-5
ISBN-10: 1-57243-841-x

TRIUMPH
B O O K S
CHICAGO

Patriot Way The Road to a Modern NFL Dynasty

CONTENTS

BOOK STAFF

Editor Gregory H. Lee Jr
Art Director Rena Anderson Sokolow
Designers Jerome Layman Jr., Aldona Charlton
Copy Editor Ron Driscoll
Researcher Emily Werchadlo
Photo Editor Jim Wilson
Imaging Frank Bright

REPORTERS

NICK CAFARDO, JACKIE MACMULLAN, JOHN POWERS,
DAN SHAUGHNESSY, MICHAEL SMITH

PHOTOGRAPHERS

JIM DAVIS Cover (Brady, Vinatieri), Inside front jacket, 6,
14, 15, 16, 18, 24, 29, 32 ,34, 37, 39, 40, 41, 47, 49, 50, 52,
57 (Kraft, Belichick), 65, 74, 77, 81, 83, 92, 94, 95, 98,
109, 110, 123, 134, 136, 139, 140, 143, 147, 148, 150, 152,
158, 165 • MATTHEW J. LEE 5, 31, 67, 68, 72, 75, 76, 79,
105, 115, 125, 132, 135, 141, 160, 161, 169, Inside back
jacket • BARRY CHIN 45, 53, 85, 89, 96, 101, 106, 108,
149, 151, 155, 157, 162, 168 (logo fans) • JOHN BOHN 21,
27, 126, 130, 163 • STAN GROSSFELD Cover (Bruschi), 51,
102, 144, 169 (sign), Back cover • BILL GREENE 54, 114,
Inside back cover • DAVID L. RYAN 56, 166 • JONATHAN
WIGGS Inside front cover • JOANNE RATHE 57 (hard hats)
• JOHN TLUMACKI 90 • MICHELE MCDONALD 112
• DOMINIC CHAVEZ 167 • ESSDRAS M SUAREZ 68 (three-
peat) • SUZANNE KREITER 169 (kids)

It's all business...

Pressure is only an illusion. To feel it you have to believe it, accept it. Pressure doesn't exist if you're a New England Patriot. It's simply not allowed. How else do you explain a team that accomplished more in a year than most NFL teams hope to accomplish in a half-century? You say win streak, they say, "What streak?" You speak of dynasty, they speak of the next foe. They conquer opponent after opponent with class and mash, the reflection of a coach with more mantras than a Hindu wise man. Football is discipline; pressure is not an option. These Patriots are indeed human. It's the Super Bowls, record winning streaks, and home invincibility that make them appear superhuman. Carrying the weight of history through the season could have slowed them down. It didn't.

year after year.

2001 An unlikely turnaround, from last place to first. 2003 After a year away, Pats climb back to mountaintop. 2004 Repeat performance: Patriots go back-to-back and seal dynasty status.

THE TRUE MEANING OF TEAM

CHAPTER ONE

9-7

They upgraded at every position, so now they can say they are an average team (as opposed to the NFL Europe team they were last year). They'll win two that they shouldn't — including vs. the Rams — and lose one they should win (Panthers?). But you'll like watching them, and you'll love the wild-card gift they're going to give you for Christmas. **MICHAEL HOLLEY**

7-9

They have a veteran defense that will keep them in games. If they get any momentum from their offense, they could surpass this win total. If they accumulate injuries on defense, they'll be worse. They have no chance of beating top teams, but because of parity, they'll be competitive with the rest of the pack. **NICK CAFARDO**

8-8

Nearly every team in the league is in the middle of the pack, so why not the Patriots? If they open 2-0 and end up 3-1 in September with Bledsoe still in one piece, they can get to 8-8 without even being .500 the rest of the year. How inconceivable is that? It's not as hard as conceiving of the Giants in last year's Super Bowl. **RON BORGES**

FINAL **11-5**

Regular Season

Cincinnati Bengals
New York Jets
Indianapolis Colts
Miami Dolphins
San Diego Chargers
Indianapolis Colts
Denver Broncos
Atlanta Falcons
Buffalo Bills
St. Louis Rams
New Orleans Saints
New York Jets
Cleveland Browns
Buffalo Bills
Miami Dolphins
Carolina Panthers

Postseason

Oakland Raiders
Pittsburgh Steelers
St. Louis Rams

01

Bengals

For openers, a botched job

17 - 23

NE	0	10	0	7
CIN	0	10	13	0

CINCINNATI

In a rather still postgame locker room, Patriots defensive lineman Bobby Hamilton let out an agonizing scream as he sat in the chair near his locker, sending vibrations through the concrete walls.

It was the only "quote" needed after New England's 23-17 loss to the Cincinnati Bengals in the season opener before 51,521 at Paul Brown Stadium on a hot, humid day.

Frustration was dripping like sweat from one corner of the spacious visiting locker room to the other.

The game was an exercise in what-ifs for the Patriots. Would they have won if they had stopped Corey Dillon (24 carries for 104 yards)? If they hadn't allowed so many big plays (a 40-yard run by Dillon and a 25-yard touchdown by tight end Tony McGee the biggest)? If they had taken advantage of play-calling by Bengals offensive coordinator Bob Bratkowski that often left observers scratching their heads? If a few close calls went their way? If they hadn't been no-shows in the third quarter? If Drew Bledsoe had made a fourth-and-2 with a quarterback sneak in the fourth quarter?

If they had done at least some of those things, they would have been 1-0. Instead, the beginning of their schedule, which had 2-0 written all over it, could end up the reverse.

"We came out weakly in the second half and we left our defense on the field way too long," said Patriots wide receiver Troy Brown, who caught seven passes for 106 yards and a touchdown.

"We had a lot of time to get it done, and we couldn't. There are going to be close calls, but it wasn't the refs' fault. We couldn't get going in the third quarter. It's our fault."

"I had too many plays I wished I could have back," said defensive co-captain Bryan Cox, who started in place of Ted Johnson (hip flexor). "We showed resiliency by coming back, but I made a bonehead play letting the tight end free for a touchdown."

The Bengals, who racked up 353 yards in total offense (157 on the ground), held only a 16-10 lead late in the third quarter when they began to gather steam.

The Bengals began a 70-yard march, with quarterback Jon Kitna, who had fumbled deep in Patriots territory in the first quarter, at one point looking down the middle of the field. There was McGee, wide open, and Kitna found him for the 25-yard score. That made it 23-10 and left Patriots defenders pointing fingers at one another on the field.

"I didn't expect to be that wide open," said McGee. "The ball was up there hanging in midair, and you have to make those plays."

Cox, who has said he no longer is good in coverage, knew how bad it looked. "I can do better," he said. "I'm not offering any excuses. Losing any game hurts, but I was the invisible man in the first half. I can't afford to be cautious. I have to look in the mirror and say that was not a good performance."

Jets

Bledsoe suffers KO; record falls to 0-2

10-3

NYJ	0	3	7	0
NE	3	0	0	0

FOXBOROUGH
When Bill Parcells coached the Patriots, he often said, "You are what you are." If you were 0-2, then you were 0-2.

But even though the 2001 Patriots are 0-2 and quarterback Drew Bledsoe was carted out on a stretcher after the game with a mild concussion, making what they are seem evident, the team believes it is better than that.

How do these players figure that? They just do.

"The team really deserved better today," said New England coach Bill Belichick, who did admonish his squad for its four turnovers in a 10-3 loss to the New York Jets in the home opener at Foxboro Stadium.

Certainly, had Marc Edwards not fumbled twice, and had Bledsoe not thrown an interception in the end zone to wreck what could have been a game-turning drive, the results might have been different. But then again... There were uplifting pregame and halftime ceremonies in tribute to the victims of the Sept. 11 terrorist attacks, and to the firefighters and policemen who aided in the rescue efforts at the World Trade Center in New York City.

While the Patriots seemed on an emotional high at the start, they couldn't get the job done.

Bledsoe wasn't able to come out for the final series, because at 4:48 of the fourth quarter he sustained a brutal sideline hit by Mo Lewis, which knocked Bledsoe unconscious for a few seconds.

Bledsoe was taken by ambulance to Massachusetts General Hospital for observation after the game, and a source close to Bledsoe said he had a mild concussion.

Another source said Bledsoe had sore ribs that may be cracked.

"I shouldn't have put him out there," said Belichick of Bledsoe, who did return for one series after the hit. "Watching him play, he wasn't himself. He got his bell rung. When I went over to him he seemed coherent and said he was OK. But after watching him I didn't think he was. I told him what decision I had made. He understood."

Bledsoe stood on the sideline rooting for backup Tom Brady, who took over with 2:16 left at the Patriots' 26.

Brady made a couple of first downs — a 21-yard pass to David Patten being the longest gain — but a pair of passes toward the end zone on the game's last two plays didn't connect.

Drew Bledsoe was briefly unconscious after a fourth-quarter hit.

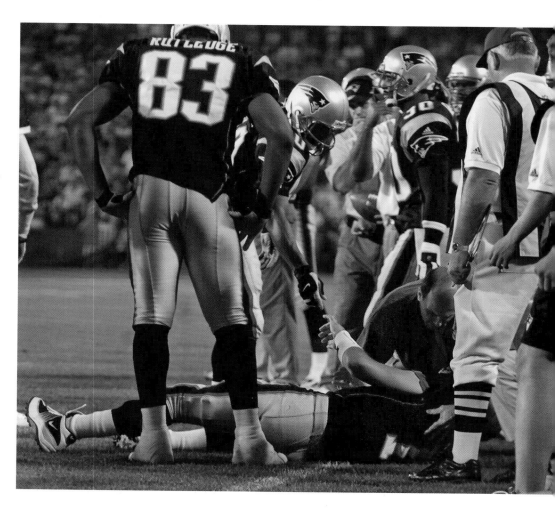

"We've got a lot of games to play and there are signs that we can compete," said linebacker Bryan Cox. "We've just got to look at the film and digest. They ain't going to cancel the season." While Cox saw signs of hope, there were certainly pockets of concern as well.

Defensive end Bobby Hamilton couldn't figure out why the defense struggled in the third quarter.

"We practiced all week playing 60 minutes of football," said Hamilton. "That was in our heads all week. We do some good things and then we have that problem." ⬭

Colts

Hold your horses; Manning muffled

44-13

IND	0	0	7	6
NE	7	13	3	21

FOXBOROUGH

When you're 0-2 and you play football in New England, you have to expect the ugly chatter to begin. The comment heard most often last week was, "Why did Bob Kraft hire Bill Belichick?"

Following a 44-13 upset win over the Indianapolis Colts in Week 3, people who asked that got their answer.

Belichick and defensive coordinator Romeo Crennel have been able to shut down Colts quarterback Peyton Manning, the most prominent offensive weapon in the division, the conference, and perhaps the league, as well as any coaching tandem in the NFL.

Without that happening, the

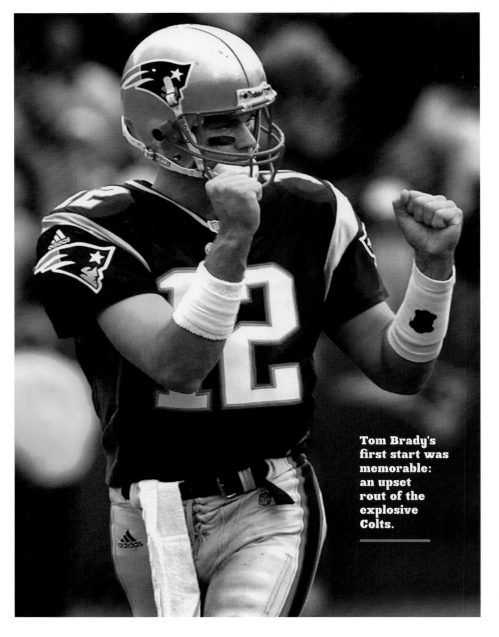

Tom Brady's first start was memorable: an upset rout of the explosive Colts.

Patriots, who improved to 1-2, might have been 0-3 and heading into oblivion. Now there is at least some hope.

While the New England offense was capably handled by second-year quarterback Tom Brady, with the injured Drew Bledsoe on the sideline holding play sheets after spending most of the week with a tube in his chest at Massachusetts General Hospital, Belichick's defense froze the Colts' Big Three.

Manning, now 0-4 at Foxboro Stadium, was 20 for 34 with 196 yards, one touchdown, and three interceptions. Edgerrin James ran 17 times for 55 yards. Marvin Harrison caught only three passes for 49 yards, with no touchdowns.

It was almost a complete role reversal by the teams. But this was more than the Patriots finding a needle in a haystack. They beat up the Colts in every way, shape, and manner possible.

"It was hard to move the ball downfield when you can't throw on third down," said Manning, who was victimized by several dropped balls as hits by linebacker Bryan Cox and safety Lawyer Milloy seemed to create some fear in the Colts receivers.

"They rushed three guys the whole time and dropped eight guys. That's a lot of guys to throw against. It's hard to get the big play," said Manning, who had two of his interceptions run back for touchdowns, by Otis Smith and Ty Law.

While statistics often don't tell the whole story, they told everything about yesterday's game.

The Patriots had 177 yards rushing (4.5 a carry), led by Antowain Smith's 94 yards on 22 carries (he had two of the team's three rushing touchdowns) and exhibited run-blocking not seen here in some time.

Brady didn't turn the ball over, made a few key first downs, and just when it seemed as though the Colts might come back, Brady connected on two quick hits early in the fourth quarter (17 yards to David Patten, 38 yards to Antowain Smith) that led to the score that broke Indianapolis's back.

In what may be the best half they have played under Belichick, the Patriots were dominant in taking a 20-0 lead into intermission.

What happened?

For one thing, when you start with a gusting wind at your back, as the Colts did, and don't score, that usually spells trouble. But the Patriots never allowed the Colts' passing game to get

on track.

And when was the last time the Patriots accumulated 141 yards rushing in a half?

Smith had a 39-yard burst in the first quarter, on beautiful blocks by Matt Light on the left side and Damien Woody on the right. Smith capped the drive on the next play with a 4-yard run with 4:23 remaining.

"My job," said Woody, who shrugged off a stiff neck, "was to hit anybody in my way. Nothing fancy about it. Antowain made a cut off my block and then he did the rest." ⌀

Dolphins
Generous Pats wilt under Miami heat

NE	7	3	0	0
MIA	7	10	10	3

M I A M I

They said it all week and said it again and again on game day: Last week was last week.

Sure it wasn't last millennium?

The New England Patriots who routed the Indianapolis Colts Sept. 30 in Foxborough must have stayed there. The ones who fumbled away their first two games of the season showed up seven days later at Pro Player Stadium.

Everything New England did so right against the Colts, and everything it needed to do to beat the defending AFC East champion Dolphins, was missing, while so many of the breakdowns that led to 19 losses in 27 previous games resurfaced. The result was a 30-10 slapping around.

The Patriots couldn't run the ball and couldn't stop the run. They couldn't pass and couldn't stop the pass. They forced one turnover. The Dolphins collected three, and their defense was the one that scored.

New England is 1-3 and back where it was two weeks ago and where it has been so often these past few years: the drawing board.

"We got our butt handed to us," said safety Lawyer Milloy, repeating a popular refrain throughout the locker room. "We can't be one-hit wonders. We can't be good one week, collectively as a team, then come out and do what we did today. That's not how you become successful.

"It's unacceptable. They pretty much dictated the game."

It made for an especially difficult afternoon for novice quarterback Tom Brady. After being asked to do very little and doing that very well against the Colts, Brady played his age in his second pro start and second relief appearance for Drew Bledsoe, completing 12 of 24 passes for a mere 86 yards with no touchdowns and no interceptions.

Why the difference? Well, for starters, there was Jason Taylor rushing from his blind side. Then there were Sam Madison and Patrick Surtain on the backs of Troy Brown and David Patten like jersey numbers. And, most important, the Patriots ran for just 80 yards on 23 carries, meaning Brady, for the first time, was asked to carry an offense.

"We didn't do enough to make him comfortable," said Brown, who put up tight-end-type numbers with five receptions for 47 yards and muffed a punt that set up an Olindo Mare 19-yard field goal in the second quarter. "We didn't make enough plays for him. He's in a tough situation."

Rather than comment specifically on Brady's performance, coach Bill

Adam Vinatieri's reward for the winning FG vs. San Diego? A tackle by teammate Lonie Paxton.

Belichick emphasized instead that the entire offensive unit was to blame for the debacle. The Patriots gained 149 yards on 51 plays, an average of 2.9 yards.

"Offensively we broke down in a lot of different areas, not just one," Belichick said. "We need to refocus and regenerate our efforts toward being a more efficient football team — not turning the ball over, not having penalties that cost us field position, not giving the other team opportuni-

ties that just make it harder for us to win. ... We can't donate stuff to opponents. We're too generous."

The game effectively ended when, working deep in Patriots territory with the team trailing, 20-10, and two minutes to go in the third quarter, Brady fumbled the snap from center Damien Woody at the 14. Brady kicked the ball backward, Taylor scooped it up at the 1, and...

"Instead of being down by 10, you're down by 17," Woody said. ✐

Chargers
Brady-led rally erases errors

29 - 26

SD	3	3	7	13	0
NE	3	6	7	10	3

FOXBOROUGH

It could be said that all the good that happened to New England in its 29-26 overtime victory over the San Diego Chargers came after Lee Johnson committed one of the most horrific blunders in recent Patriots' history.

Back to punt deep in his own territory, Johnson fielded the snap, then saw the Chargers' Derrick Harris bearing down on him.

Unable to get the punt off, Johnson quickly was in Harris's grasp, then held the ball in his left hand, away from his body, until he lost it.

Harris scooped up the loose ball at the Patriots' 6-yard line and rumbled into the end zone for the score, giving San Diego, which trailed a minute and a half earlier, a 26-16 lead with 8:48 to play.

"I was still trying to punt it," said the New England punter. "When he spun me around, I realized I wasn't going to kick the ball."

Ten points behind with less than nine minutes to go, what were the Patriots to do?

"We let it go," said defensive end Bobby Hamilton.

They let go the misery and the embarrassment. They let go any concern about being 1-4, and instead are 2-3 with their upcoming three games on the road.

So Doug Flutie's farewell visit to Foxboro Stadium was a rare sour note. Flutie came in with a 12-1 record at the stadium, but he was unable to drive the Chargers for a score at the end of regulation or the beginning of overtime.

In an interesting juxtaposition, it was young Tom Brady, 15 years Flutie's junior, playing the role of pigskin magician.

He pulled a few rabbits out of the hat, leading the Patriots to 13 points in less than 13 minutes, distributing the ball in pressure situations like a savvy veteran while ersatz quarterbacks coach Drew Bledsoe watched on the sideline. Under Brady's direction, the Patriots amassed 30 first downs and 374 total yards, with the rookie throwing for 364. They converted 7 of 15 third-down plays.

The return of Terry Glenn, who caught seven passes for 110 yards, including a second-quarter 21-yard touchdown on a pretty toss from Brady, also gave the team a boost.

"Terry makes a huge difference to our offense," said Troy Brown, who had 11 catches for 117 yards.

After the Chargers went three and out at the start of overtime, the Patriots started the winning drive at their 23.

The big play was a 37-yard interference penalty on Chargers cornerback Alex Molden, who held David Patten.

On the play, Brady, who completed 33 of 54 passes with a pair of touchdowns, called an audible, something he had practiced repeatedly but didn't figure to use.

"We talked during the week that if they ran a certain blitz, we'd audible out," said Brady. "David fought for the ball, which drew the call. The most important thing there was that we executed what we'd practiced."

The penalty advanced the ball to the Chargers 32, and Adam Vinatieri's 44-yard field goal won the game.

Throughout the game, and particularly on this drive, San Diego's vaunted blitzes were ineffective, as the Patriots' offensive line and backs did a superb job of holding back Junior Seau and Rodney Harrison.

Asked about the call, Chargers coach Mike Riley said, "It was close and when it's close like that, you don't know. They got wrapped up and when that happens you have a chance of getting that call."

Colts

Early and often, a Patten develops

38-17

NE	7	21	3	7
IND	3	3	11	0

INDIANAPOLIS

Patriots owner Robert Kraft may have to call for a special session of the re-alignment committee to reconsider Indianapolis moving out of the AFC East next season.

The Patriots don't want the Colts going anywhere.

In their last meeting as divisional opponents, the Patriots pulverized the Colts, 38-17, before a stunned RCA Dome crowd of 56,022.

Any thoughts of the Colts getting revenge were squashed in the first 30 minutes, when the Patriots blocked two field-goal attempts and their offense exploded for a 28-6 lead. Wide receiver David Patten put forth an incredible performance by running for a touchdown, catching two, and passing for one. All but the second TD reception came before halftime.

Suddenly a team that was having trouble climbing out of the AFC East cellar is 3-3 and right in the mix.

The Patriots, who beat the Colts, 44-13, in Week 3 at Foxboro Stadium, outscored Indianapolis, 82-30, in their final series as division rivals. (The Colts will be part of the new AFC South starting in 2002.)

New England also posted its first road win of the season; entering the game, the Patriots had lost 14 of their last 16 away games.

"It was just so much fun out there,"

said the Patriots' Tom Brady, who enjoyed a quarterback rating of 148.3, the second-highest of the game (Patten had a 158.3 for his 60-yard TD pass to Troy Brown). Brady completed 16 of 20 passes for 202 yards with three scores and has thrown 131 passes without being intercepted.

"Just to be able to try different plays and see them working like that makes it interesting," he said. "Our special teams made a couple of big plays and our defense was awesome. It was a game I hope the fans enjoyed as much as the players."

Coach Bill Belichick spent much time during the week having his team practice special teams play. He released punter Lee Johnson, who had botched a key play against San Diego, and warned the members of the unit it was time to make plays.

They did.

On the Colts' first drive, Brandon Mitchell got a hand up and blocked Mike Vanderjagt's 46-yard field goal attempt. Rookie Leonard Myers picked up the loose ball and ran it 35 yards to the Colts' 29.

"Those were huge plays," Belichick said of the major contributions of the special teams.

One play later, offensive coordinator Charlie Weis called his first razzle-dazzle play. Brady handed the ball to Antowain Smith, who was going left, and he handed to Patten, who ran it back around right end for 29 yards for New England's first touchdown.

Vanderjagt answered with a 42-yard field goal with 5:44 remaining in the first quarter, but in the second the Patriots made history.

Starting at their 9, Brady tossed a perfect ball to Patten, who had slipped past David Macklin on a post pattern. Patten hauled it in and used his speed to finish the 91-yard touchdown. It was the longest play from scrimmage in

Patriots history.

"It was one of those days when everything was clicking," said Patten, who produced 226 yards — four catches for 117 yards, the throw for 60, the run for 29 yards, and a kickoff return for 20 yards. "Every time I touched the ball, I was able to make something happen. That's what I pride myself on. I think I'm able to do that every time I go on the field, and today I made it happen."

Broncos

A quarter to forget: four interceptions

20 - 31

NE	10	7	3	0
DEN	7	3	14	7

DENVER

It was the Brady Bunch — four interceptions in the fourth quarter — that contributed to the Patriots' 31-20 loss to the Broncos.

To blame it all on quarterback Tom Brady would not be fair. Troy Brown and Lawyer Milloy were more than willing to take their share of the blame, and coach Bill Belichick said Brady played well.

When he didn't play well was in crunch time.

After the Broncos had taken a 24-20 lead with two unanswered scores, Brady needed to rally the troops, and he failed.

"I'm the guy who needs to make those plays," said Brady, who had four of his last 11 passes intercepted after not being picked off in the first 162 of his career. "No excuses. I've just got to

get better, and I will."

Milloy said a breakdown in the secondary occurred when Rod Smith was allowed to cross over the middle, catch a Brian Griese pass at the 40, and race down the sideline for a 65-yard score, cutting the Patriots' lead to 20-17 with 10:35 remaining in the third quarter.

"There was miscommunication on the coverage, and that's inexcusable," said Milloy. "For Smith to beat us like that, that's hard to swallow. We were doubling him and I was the safety helping out over the top. It was a quick crossing play and the corner thought I was going to be somewhere else. It's our job as a defense to put Tom in a stress-free situation and we didn't do it."

The Denver defense then started coming hard at Brady. The Broncos sacked him twice on the next series, which was a three-and-out. The Broncos took over at their 20 and marched 80 yards as Griese again beat out Brady, just like in their University of Michigan days when Griese won the starting job. He hooked up with tight end Dwayne Carswell for a 6-yard touchdown with 3:35 left in the third. That gave Denver a 24-20 lead.

The big play on that drive was another Patriots defensive blunder, this one by Matt Stevens, who overpursued tight end Desmond Clark, went past him, and allowed Clark to get off the ground without touching him, making it a 35-yard gain.

"The whistle didn't blow," said Belichick. "It was an alert play by them and a not-so-alert play by us."

Brady's first big mistake came when he tried to get the ball to David Patten in the end zone early in the fourth quarter. Brady, under pressure, threw off-balance and Denard Walker picked it off, deflating New England's spirit after it had driven from its 22 to the Broncos 13.

Kevin Faulk's TD catch helped the Patriots beat Atlanta and improve to .500 for the season.

Falcons

At halfway point, the glass is half-full

24-10

NE	0	17	7	0
ATL	7	0	0	3

On the Patriots' next series, Brady threw from his 49 to the Broncos 19, but Deltha O'Neal was there to pick it off over Patten. And after the defense held the Broncos again, Brady tossed one into no-man's land, a ball Walker picked off and ran in 39 yards for the final score.

"I take most of the blame for the loss," said Brown, the intended receiver on the play. "I was out there reading the defensive back and I didn't get on the same page. He threw it to the outside and I went to the inside. My fault."

A T L A N T A
Beating the Atlanta Falcons, 24-10, in Week 8 does not warrant a parade. But when one considers where the Patriots came from, and where they now stood, making it to .500 at the halfway point of the season is a major accomplishment.

They achieved a 4-4 mark by winning two of three consecutive road games, no small feat in a league in which most teams don't play well away from home.

The players were happy and positive, sensing a legitimate opportunity at the playoffs.

With significant contributors Drew Bledsoe, Terry Glenn, and Bryan Cox sidelined by injuries, the Patriots did what they've wanted to do since the season started: play 60 intense minutes. It is a simple concept, but a difficult task.

Certainly New England possessed a bit of luck on Troy Brown's 44-yard catch that bounced off a Falcons defender and went for a touchdown in

2001

Antowain Smith became the first New England back with a 1,000-yard season in three years, rushing for 1,157 yards.

2003

The Patriots rushed for only 3.4 yards per carry, which ranked 30th in the NFL.

POSTSEASON 210 yards rushing in 2004 against Colts was first

2004
Corey Dillon broke the team's season rushing record with a 1,635-yard performance.

time in Super Bowl run that they ran for more yards than they passed for.

All at once, Antowain Smith celebrated a 42-yard TD run, a 100-yard game, and a win over his former team, the Bills.

the third quarter to seal the win. But it was the never-waning intensity that was most responsible for the result.

The Patriots sacked Chris Chandler and Michael Vick nine times, and allowed only 104 net passing yards. The Patriots' Tom Brady was 21 of 31 for 250 yards and three touchdowns.

"If you say you're going to blitz, you've got to get there," said Patriots defensive end Bobby Hamilton.

Defensive coordinator Romeo Crennel and coach Bill Belichick know that Chandler is similar in style to Bledsoe. So, as they used to do in defensing Bledsoe while coaching on other teams, they moved Willie McGinest around on the defensive line, and shot safeties and linebackers up the middle and from the edges. The Falcons never knew what hit them.

"I don't know how teams defend against us anyway," said Lawyer Milloy. "We have a different game plan every week. You can't watch film on us and figure out what we're going to do against you the following week."

And Charlie Weis's game plan was nothing short of brilliant. The offensive coordinator received accolades for his trick-play-based attack against the Colts two weeks ago, but in this game he had his work cut out for him. For one, he knew the Falcons would take away his wide receivers, Troy Brown and David Patten. Without Glenn (hamstring), Weis had to develop another look. So Brady threw to his backs (Antowain Smith, Kevin Faulk, and Marc Edwards, who combined for 10 catches and two touchdowns). ⊘

Bills
Making sure the last shall not be first

21 - 11

BUF	0	3	0	8
NE	7	0	7	7

FOXBOROUGH
The Patriots gave the Bills plenty of respect before, during, and after their 21-11 win in Week 9, which put New England over the .500 mark (5-4) for the first time since December of 1999.

The postgame news conferences were filled with praise for their 1-7 opponent, which had every opportunity to spoil the Patriots' party but couldn't come up with a big play when needed.

"We got lucky today," said Patriots receiver Troy Brown. "That's a pretty good football team."

Brown's comments may be a stretch, because the Bills are far from good. And the Patriots weren't "lucky" all the time, at times they were good.

New England running back Antowain Smith, who gained 100 yards on 20 carries with two touchdowns, got 42 of those yards with a scoring run with 1:52 remaining to eliminate any chance of the Bills pulling the game out. An Alex Van Pelt touchdown pass and conversion throw had gotten Buffalo within 14-11. Van Pelt had entered for the Bills after the Patriots knocked out a quarterback (Rob Johnson, shoulder) for the second time in an as many weeks (Atlanta's Chris Chandler, ribs, the previous week).

But then Smith shook off a missed tackle at the line of scrimmage and broke into daylight, finishing off his former teammates in a bit of poetic justice. "Guys were asking me, 'How did you get out of there?' " said Smith. "I said, 'I don't know. I broke a couple of tackles and all I could see was the end zone.' "

Young quarterback Tom Brady wasn't terrific, but he wasn't terrible, either. He got the job done, even with the Bills blitzing him often.

"You'd like to play great every week," said Brady. "But that's not the case in this league, as I'm finding out."

The Bills sacked Brady seven times, and he threw one interception and fumbled twice. All of that should have led to a Bills' win, but the Bills are 1-7 for a reason.

"I thought defensively we played extremely well all day," said Buffalo coach Gregg Williams. "Offensively we have to do a better job on third down. We have to keep the chains moving." The Bills were 2 for 12 on third-down conversions.

Despite that, the Bills pulled within 3 points shortly after Terrell Buckley sacked Johnson on a blitz on second

and 16 from the New England 25. In came Van Pelt, who threw two consecutive incompletions.

But on the Patriots' next series, Kendrick Office forced Brady to cough up the ball with a good hit as Brady was backtracking. The ball was kicked backward and recovered by Jay Foreman at the Patriots 17.

Van Pelt's first pass was thrown poorly toward Peerless Price, but on his second attempt he found Price in the end zone.

"It was a route we designed to get either Jay [Riemersma] or Peerless open," said Van Pelt. "They covered Jay with a safety and a linebacker, leaving the middle of the field open for Peerless, who did a nice job on the route and was pretty much wide open." Van Pelt's conversion pass to Eric Moulds, over Ty Law, made it 14-11 with 2:43 to play. ⊘

Rams
There's no slowing down St. Louis

17 - 24

STL	7	7	3	7
NE	7	3	0	7

FOXBOROUGH
After 60 minutes of football, it was clear. The Patriots, 24-17 losers to the St. Louis Rams in Week 10, aren't quite in the same league as the Rams. But who is?

"One thing that came out of this is that we know we're a good team," said Patriots cornerback Ty Law, who spent most of the game chasing down Rams receivers. "We had a chance to win the game, but we made too many mistakes. It's that simple."

The Rams improved to 8-1 and ended the Patriots' two-game winning streak, evening their record at 5-5. The Patriots were unable to stay in the hunt for the top spot in the AFC East, as the New York Jets defeated the Miami Dolphins, 24-0, to improve to 7-3.

Rams quarterback Kurt Warner, despite throwing a pair of interceptions and fumbling once, threw for three touchdowns and 401 yards. His New England counterpart, Tom Brady, was picked off twice and threw a touchdown pass in the fourth quarter. It was too little, too late.

"It wasn't like we weren't moving the ball," said Brady.

The Rams simply wore down the Patriots' defense. What also killed New England was a controversial play late in the second quarter inside the St. Louis 5-yard line.

Antowain Smith fumbled at the 4, and it was recovered by the Rams at the 3. The Patriots thought Smith was down before the ball popped loose, but their replay challenge failed to get the call overruled.

"I have to blame myself," said Smith. "It's not all right in that situation. I'm a veteran, I've got to have better ball security in that situation. I have to put it behind me real fast. We had an opportunity to shock the world — that turnover killed us."

The Rams turned around and marched 97 yards for a score and a 14-point swing.

"We left a lot on the field," said Patriots cornerback Otis Smith. "We had to spread our defense to match what they had to offer. We let them score, which we shouldn't do. We should never let them march 97 yards like that. That hurt."

The Patriots hung in to the end, but the Rams held the ball for the final

7:46, converting three third downs to seal the win and taking a knee three times to end it.

The Rams' winning margin came on an 11-yard pass from Warner to fullback James Hodgins that made it 24-10 with 10:32 left.

The Patriots didn't cower, however. On their next possession, Brady put together his best series, driving the team 65 yards in 2:46. He connected on all five of his passes, the key one a 27-yarder down the middle to David Patten, who had been fairly quiet. With the ball at the Rams 21, Brady threw 11 yards to Kevin Faulk. From the 10, Brady found Patten alone in the corner of the end zone, making it 24-17 with 7:46 remaining.

Saints

Brady (4 TD passes) buries controversy

34-17

NO	0	0	10	7
NE	7	13	0	14

FOXBOROUGH
Patriots coach Bill Belichick could have stood at the podium following a 34-17 win over the New Orleans Saints and said, "I told you so." Instead, he wished his son, Brian, a happy birthday, and simply let quarterback Tom Brady's performance speak for itself.

Belichick, who created a firestorm with veteran QB Drew Bledsoe by announcing that he was staying with Brady for the game against New Orleans, received major reinforcement, as Brady threw for a career-high four touchdowns and emphatically ended

the quarterback controversy.

The Patriots improved to 6-5 and stayed in the hunt for a playoff berth by outmuscling one of the most physical teams in the league at rainy, misty Foxboro Stadium.

The Saints played as horribly as their staff coached, allowing the Patriots to convert 62 percent of their third-down plays, allowing 432 total net yards (191 on the ground), and letting Antowain Smith rush for 111 yards on 24 carries and score two touchdowns, one on a 41-yard screen pass from Brady.

"A lot of people were talking about how we were gonna respond after we lost to the Rams," said New England safety Lawyer Milloy, who had 10 tackles, one interception, and two passes defensed. "Well, I like the way this team responded. I think we're going to be a dangerous team in the latter part of the season."

For Belichick, there never was a quarterback controversy; he believed Brady had performed well enough over the previous eight games to keep the job. Brady had a quarterback rating of 143.9 vs. the Saints and threw for 258 yards, seven of the balls going to Troy Brown, who gained 91 yards. Brady also hit Brown, Marc Edwards, and Charles Johnson for scores. Bledsoe was booed by the crowd as he left the field for the tunnel, and one person held a sign that said, "Drew: Want Some Cheese with your Whine?"

"I thought they played their best football game as a team," said Belichick. "I thought the offensive line did an admirable job against a good front. It was a good win defensively."

Brady was having so much fun that late in the game he even threw a block on Saints safety Sammy Knight to spring Smith for a big gain.

He walked off the field at the half leading, 20-0, and was all smiles. He even got a smile out of Bledsoe on the sideline after he stuck a 24-yard pass to Johnson for the Patriots' third score of the half with 10 seconds remaining. That capped a 78-yard drive, in which Smith busted for runs of 12 and 11 yards and Brady found a wide-open David Patten for 27 yards to the 24.

It was amazing how open Patriots receivers often were. "They played a lot of man-to-man on us and we were able to get some receivers open," said Belichick.

The Saints blitzed at times, but most of the time the offensive line covered them. The line was much more physical than New Orleans.

"That was a tough defensive front four," said center Damien Woody. "We knew coming in that we would have to be as physical as they were and even more to win the game." ◯

Jets

Giving no quarter, taking the 2nd half

17-16

NE	0	0	14	3
NYJ	10	3	3	0

EAST RUTHERFORD
Even in victory, the faces of the Patriots' coaches often are stoic and stern. That's a sign of them rarely being satisfied, and never wanting to let their players know when they are satisfied. But for once, they allowed themselves to show a little emotion.

The assistant coaches in the booth adjoining the press box were applauding and screaming after every good play down the stretch. Head man Bill Belichick was hugging players, giving high-fives and slaps on the back.

"He hugged me on the field," said Patriots outside linebacker Roman Phifer following New England's 17-16, come-from-behind victory over the Jets. "I'd never got one of those from him before."

It is Belichick's (and director of player personnel Scott Pioli's) collection of nomads — Phifer, Bryan Cox, Terrell Buckley, Antowain Smith, Marc Edwards, etc. — who have made the Patriots better.

The team listened intently to Belichick's halftime speech, in which he said, "Our season is on the line. Either we get it done the last 30 minutes, or we're looking down the barrel of the New York Jets."

They responded with a huge win, and they did it patiently.

Offensive coordinator Charlie Weis began making the most of a short-to-intermediate passing game, which ultimately opened big gainers to Smith and former XFL-er Fred Coleman.

With a 7-5 record, the Patriots are right in the middle of the conference playoff chase.

In the AFC East, they trail the Dolphins (8-3) by 1½ games and the Jets (7-4) by a half-game. If the season ended now, they'd be in the playoffs.

"We discussed all week that we control our own destiny," said veteran safety Lawyer Milloy. "We saw that most of the teams we had on the schedule were around or at our record, and that if we beat them we could go

Patriots' safety Matt Stevens breaks up a pass intended for the Saints' Boo Williams.

to the playoffs."

"I don't want to talk about last year," said defensive end Bobby Hamilton, "but if they had gotten the lead against us last year, we'd have given up. We have a bunch of fighters out there. We feel we can do anything if we put our mind to it."

What looked hopeless at halftime really wasn't. The Jets scored on their first possession, and then twice had to settle for field goals when touchdowns might have put it out of reach.

"It was a tale of two halves," said linebacker Cox, who played in his first game since breaking his right fibula in two places against the Broncos Oct. 28.

"They controlled the first half, and we controlled the second half."

When exactly did the Patriots win this game? Was it Buckley's interception with 2:07 remaining at the Patriots' 33, foiling Vinny Testaverde's final drive? Was it Tom Brady's 2-yard run on third and 2 with 1:46 remaining to seal it for good? Was it Coleman's catch on a slant with 11:13 remaining in the third that went for 46 yards and set the stage for Smith's 4-yard run, trimming the Jets' lead to 13-7? Was it Mike Vrabel's third-quarter interception at the Patriots' 31 that came before those two plays?

Maybe all of the above. After Adam Vinatieri's 28-yard field goal put the Patriots in the lead for the first and final time at 6:29 of the fourth quarter, the Jets had plenty of time to win it. Tebucky Jones, who was terrific on special teams all day, made a nice tackle on kick returner Craig Yeast at the 25. The Jets made a pair of first downs and were at the Patriots' 45 with 2:54 remaining. But the New England defense was relentless: Matt Stevens blitzed on third and 5 and forced Testaverde out of the pocket. He rolled right but was forced to dump the pass. On fourth and 5, the Jets'

last chance, Buckley stepped in front of tight end Anthony Becht and intercepted to end the threat.

"We put an extra guy in on that play," said Buckley. "You knew they were going to pass. We just had to get our coverage guys in there."

Brady's late run was significant because Belichick said the quarterback was in pain from a shot he'd taken in the ribs, and because Brady was somewhat skeptical.

"I asked the coach if he was sure, and Drew [Bledsoe] said, 'Just run the ball, get the first down, and win the game,' " said Brady.

Brady, who finished 20 for 28 for 213 yards with no touchdowns or interceptions, said of his team not scoring in the first half, "We just didn't move the ball. When we had a chance to extend a drive [they were 1 for 6 converting third downs] we didn't. It goes to show it's a 60-minute game, and it's not over after two quarters."

Browns

Taking playoff chase one game at a time

27-16

CLE	10	0	3	3
NE	3	17	0	7

FOXBOROUGH
Robert Kraft was smiling, shaking hands, and greeting fans at Foxboro Stadium, but he was not about to get carried away over the fortunes of his New England Patriots following their latest triumph, a 27-16 win over the Cleveland Browns.

Not yet, anyway.

All hands signal an Antowain Smith TD plunge against the Browns.

"One week at a time," said the Patriots owner. "One week at a time."

Carefully and conservatively, the Patriots measured and calculated what was ahead. From Kraft down to the 53d player, nobody wanted to take the leap that so many are making — that the Patriots, barring a disastrous col-

lapse, will be in the playoffs.

"One step closer," said running back Antowain Smith. "We're one step closer."

"One slip, and we're sitting home in January," cautioned Ty Law.

The Patriots, who improved to 8-5, struggled at times to put away the Browns, needing four turnovers and several big plays. But they again remained focused, winning their third straight and fifth in six weeks.

The Browns trailed New England by only a half-game in the wild-card chase entering the game, so it was critical for both teams. The Patriots also wanted to make the Browns pay for some of the trash-talking they did after beating New England last season, one of Cleveland's three wins.

"They're big talkers," said Law, "and the quotes we heard from them after last year's game, we didn't appreciate them. We knew they didn't respect us.

They were boasting about beating the Patriots. That's not good."

Big plays? There was a fourth-quarter pooch punt by Adam Vinatieri, coupled with a nice play by Jermaine Wiggins to keep the ball out of the end zone, that pinned Cleveland at its 2. The ensuing Browns punt left the Patriots with great field position, and they converted with a touchdown that iced the game.

There was a big third-down run by Smith, who was contained much of the day, to help the Patriots run out the clock, and an 85-yard punt return for a touchdown by Troy Brown.

Then there was the return of Terry Glenn, who caught four passes for 67 yards, and an overall toughness by the Patriots, which is becoming the team's trademark.

It all adds up to a feeling that the playoffs are in the Patriots' future. At 8-5, they have games at Buffalo (next week) and Carolina, two of the league's weak sisters. In between is a home game against Miami, which leads the AFC East at 8-3 entering tonight's home game against the Colts.

Tom Brady played a bit more like the novice he is, throwing two interceptions, but he completed 19 of 28 passes for 218 yards and kept his composure when it mattered most.

The Patriots held a 20-10 halftime lead, but Cleveland cut it to 20-16 with 12:39 to play on the second of Phil Dawson's second-half field goals.

With just less than 10 minutes to go, the Patriots defense, which did not allow a touchdown (Corey Fuller's interception return and three Dawson field goals accounted for Cleveland's scoring), forced a turnover.

Cleveland took a 10-3 lead in the first quarter when Fuller picked off Brady and raced 49 yards for the TD.

Brady wasn't fazed by the interception. As he often has done, Brady an-

swered a poor possession with a good one. Starting at their 34, Brady and the Patriots marched down the field, converting four first downs. Smith, who converted a fourth-and-1 play from the 3, scored from the 1 to tie it, 10-10, with 9:39 left in the half.

A third-down sack by Phifer forced the Browns to punt with 3:45 to go. Brown caught Chris Gardocki's punt at the 15, and received two big blocks, onefrom Lawyer Milloy on Dwayne Rudd, the other by Richard Seymour on Gardocki. Brown did the rest. ⊘

Bills

On further review, Pats keep the ball

12 - 9

NE	3	3	0	3	3
BUF	0	0	3	6	0

ORCHARD PARK, NY David Patten was unconscious, lying on the cold Ralph Wilson Stadium turf, his head out of bounds, the rest of his body inbounds. The ball was beneath his legs after safety Keion Carpenter had blasted him following a 13-yard reception from Tom Brady.

It was 9-9 in overtime in a divisional game that meant everything to the Patriots, and much less to the Bills, but Buffalo jerseys came flying out of nowhere toward the loose ball, and Nate Clements grabbed it.

It appeared Patten had fumbled after making a catch at the Buffalo 41. Patten was unconscious for approximately 10 seconds, and when he finally came to, the officials were running around, and the Bills were claiming

they'd recovered a fumble.

When the replay official reviewed the play, he invoked Rule 3, Section 20, Article 2, Paragraph C of the rule book.

Referee Mike Carey said, "On the play, there is a reception by the receiver. He fumbled. The ball was loose in the field of play and while in contact with the receiver's calf, his head hit out of bounds. By rule, that's a loose ball. If a loose ball touches anything that is out of bounds, it is itself out of bounds and it would be in possession of the receiver."

The Patriots retained possession, and went on to an amazing 12-9 win on Adam Vinatieri's 23-yard field goal, his fourth of the game. The kick was set up by a 38-yard Antowain Smith run on which he bounced off three would-be tacklers and broke into the clear.

The Patriots improved to 9-5 with their fourth straight win, setting the stage for a showdown with the Dolphins, with first place in the AFC East on the line, in Week 15 at Foxboro Stadium.

But nobody was ready to speak about the Dolphins.

"I'll think about them Tuesday," said linebacker Bryan Cox. "We're going to enjoy this one right now."

And there were sighs of relief. After all, four of the Patriots' last five games against the Bills have gone to overtime.

"We know how fortunate we are to come out of here with a win," said Smith, who for the second time this season buried his former team with a long run in the last minutes of the game. "It was just one of those things. I got stopped in a pile of people, kept my legs moving, and bounced away. You never give up. I hadn't contributed like I wanted the entire game. The Bills are a tough team defensively and

Ty Law cuts in front of Buffalo's Eric Moulds to make an interception in the second quarter.

they've shown that in two games. To win this, we're so happy."

The win — and the favorable call by the officials — made the Patriots look more and more like a team of destiny.

"I really don't know what the ruling was," said coach Bill Belichick. "Mike came over to explain it and I couldn't even hear him. We were trying to get the rest of the plays in at that point."

Bills coach Gregg Williams called it a "tough call." He added, "I was told that the ball was fumbled and the ball was in contact with the team that last possessed it. So they ruled out of bounds by contact. I have never seen a play like that."

Patten said, "In training camp when the officials came to visit us for their yearly review of rules, they showed us a similar play."

their support.

"This was," said Phifer, pausing to collect himself, "the most important game of my life. It's the first time in 11 years that I'll be going to the playoffs. I can't tell you what that means to me. I can't tell you how I feel right now because it's a feeling I don't think I've experienced."

While the AFC East-leading Patriots (10-5) haven't officially qualified for the playoffs, it would take a miracle for New England to miss the postseason.

In fact, even if the Patriots lose to Carolina, the Seattle Seahawks, who have three games remaining, would have to win all three and outscore their final two conference opponents (San Diego and Kansas City) by more than 58 points to keep the Patriots out.

"What a coaching job Bill has done," said Phifer, a Jets castoff and former Ram who was wooed in the off-season by Belichick and player personnel director Scott Pioli. "You appreciate it from the outside, but in here it's amazing to watch week after week."

The Patriots not only overtook the Dolphins, they sent a message to the league that they're capable of beating any team.

They received an outstanding performance from Tebucky Jones, whose jarring tackles forced two tide-turning fumbles.

They were able to run the ball at will, a reversal of the teams' Oct. 7 meeting in Miami when Lamar Smith blitzed the New England defense for 144 yards. This time, another Smith, New England's Antowain, ran for a

Dolphins

Tables are turned, statement is made

20-13

MIA	0	3	0	10
NE	0	20	0	0

FOXBOROUGH

Roman Phifer watched as teammates poured a Gatorade bucket of ice water over Bill Belichick's head near the conclusion of their 20-13 victory over the Miami Dolphins. He then joined his teammates for an impromptu run around the stadium to thank fans for

Guard Mike Compton drops in on Patrick Pass after Pass's TD catch vs. Miami.

career-high 156 yards on 26 carries and a touchdown.

Tom Brady threw for 108 yards and snapped a three-game touchdown drought with a 23-yard scoring toss to Patrick Pass.

The offensive line was dominant, opening holes for Smith and taking Jason Taylor, the Dolphins' vaunted pass rusher, out of the game.

"It really helped us that we got the ground game going, because that meant we didn't have to pass protect as much," said left tackle Matt Light.

The defense hadn't allowed a touchdown in 14 quarters before Jay Fiedler connected with Jeff Ogden on a 10-yard pass with 1:28 remaining. The Dolphins attempted an onside kick, which happens to be Olindo Mare's specialty, and the high kick fell into the arms of Fred Coleman, just as a truck named David Bowens drilled the Patriot receiver in the midsection.

But Coleman held the ball.

"I figure I'm going to get hit anyway so I'd might as well catch the ball," said Coleman. "And he hit me good. He hit me right on the ball, so I had to readjust it as I came down."

The Dolphins had many opportunities to come back from a 20-3 halftime deficit, but were foiled at every turn.

The first came on their first drive of the second half. Faced with fourth and 1 at the New England 21-yard line, the Dolphins went to Smith, who tried to go over the top on the right side. Smith, however, was stuffed by Matt Stevens and Tedy Bruschi, giving the Patriots possession after the biggest stop of the game.

Certainly there was questionable play-calling by Miami offensive coordinator Chan Gailey. The Patriots had loaded up the box on fourth down, but instead of throwing to a tight end, the Dolphins decided to try and outmuscle the Patriots. But that hasn't happened

very often this year, and it didn't happen this time.

Ironically, the same thing had happened to the Patriots on the first drive of the game. Brady led the team from its 38 to the Miami 10. Faced with fourth and 1, Belichick eschewed a gimme field goal and Antowain Smith was stuffed.

"That's one I wish we could have taken back," said Belichick. "Taylor knocked down [Marc] Edwards and took us out of the play."

Panthers
Clinching effort, and a 1st-round bye

38 - 6

NE	10	0	14	14
CAR	0	3	3	0

CHARLOTTE

The Patriots took part in all the usual division-clinching activities after their 38-6 victory over the Carolina Panthers, which gave them the AFC East title for the first time since 1997.

They donned championship caps and T-shirts. Otis Smith and Lawyer Milloy dropped a bucketful of ice water over coach Bill Belichick's head. Players threw parts of their uniforms to Patriots fans, who made up an estimated 40 percent of the 21,070 on hand in the cold, drizzly conditions.

And they presented the game ball to defensive coordinator Romeo Crennel, whose mother died during the week.

Owner Robert Kraft shook hands with and waved to fans, enjoying a moment he probably thought wouldn't come so soon in the Belichick era.

Chief operating officer Andy Wasynczuk pumped his fist and walked quietly toward the team bus.

"For the next three hours, let's root for the Jets," said Kraft, who thanked all of the New England fans at Ericsson Stadium, some of whom drove 14 hours to the game.

Whether the rooting helped or not, the Jets beat the Raiders a few hours after New England's win, and, as a result, the Patriots, who went from 5-11 last season (Belichick's first) to 11-5 this season, are the No. 2 seed in the AFC playoffs and have a first-round bye this weekend. They'll host a second-round game at Foxboro Stadium Jan. 19 or 20.

Perhaps linebacker Tedy Bruschi summed it up best, even though he suffered a concussion during the second quarter and had to leave the game.

The cobwebs lifted, and his eyes refocused, Bruschi said, "You can win 16 games in a row, and then lose the first game of the playoffs. What good is that? That's why we have to enjoy what we've done for a while, and then we'd better get back to work with the same concentration and focus we've had to get here."

The Patriots forced six Carolina turnovers, with Ty Law and Smith returning interceptions for touchdowns of 46 and 76 yards.

Law's return gave the Patriots a 10-0 lead and some steam. He stepped in front of intended receiver Steve Smith and was off to the races, some Panthers giving up on the play.

"We knew the traction wasn't that good and that the receivers would have trouble coming out of their breaks," said Law. "That was one of those situations."

Still, the Patriots led only 10-3 at the half against the Panthers, who set an NFL record with their 15th straight loss this season. Any Carolina upset thoughts were dashed quickly in the second half, when Troy Brown fielded a 61-yard punt by Pro Bowler Todd Sauerbrun and returned it 68 yards, dodging three Panthers along the way, to give the Patriots a 17-3 lead with 8:30 left in the third quarter.

"I saw an opening and I hit it," said Brown, who also broke the Patriots record for catches in a season, eclipsing Ben Coates's 96. Brown had six catches for 45 yards, giving him 101 receptions for the season.

"I slipped on my first return going along the sideline, so I decided to go up the middle," Brown said. "When you have a chance to make a play like that to help your team get out in front and change momentum, you try your best to hit it. I got big blocks up front and I just hit the middle full speed. I wasn't stopping. When I came through the pack, I saw the punter. I had to make the punter miss." ⌀

After a 1-3 start, the Patriots went 10-2 to secure their first AFC East division title since 1997.

ENGLAND TEAM RECORD WITH 101 RECEPTIONS AND LEADS THE AFC IN PUNT RETURNS.

BY JACKIE MACMULLAN

NOT OVER YET

AFTER A 1-3 START, THE SEASON QUICKLY CHANGED FOR SURGING PATRIOTS

The New England Patriots' season started when Drew Bledsoe's ended.

When the three-time Pro Bowl quarterback went down in a near-fatal heap after New York Jets linebacker Mo Lewis blasted him late in the second game of an already bizarre season, it seemed all might be lost even before much of anything had begun.

Explosive wide receiver Terry Glenn was already suspended for at least a month and threatening to sue all of New England, if necessary, to get his bonus money back; the offensive line was recovering from having been a tattered mess of injuries for most of the exhibition season; Bledsoe had just suffered a chest injury so severe he would lose more than 7 pints of blood twice in the ensuing 24 hours; the country was reeling from a terrorist attack; the team had lost two straight to the Bengals and Jets; their quarterbacks coach had died in shocking fashion a month earlier; their highest-paid defensive lineman was still suffering from the effects of offseason back surgery; and the guy replacing Bledsoe had completed exactly one pass in his brief NFL career.

As starts go, it wasn't much, but it's not where you start in the National Football League that counts. It's where you finish, and the Patriots were far from finished, even though they seemed so that afternoon of Sept. 23 when Bledsoe went down.

It was a day already tinged with tragedy, the first day the NFL returned to the field after the terrorist attacks of Sept. 11.

As part of the world changed, so did pro football. For a week no games were played.

Shocked but not stymied, the country returned to a normal way of life. That meant many things, and one was fall Sundays devoted with almost biblical faith to pro football.

Yet when the NFL returned, everything was different in a year when a lot of different things had already happened in New England. Few things at the time boded well. Certainly not for these battered Patriots.

MAKING RIGHT CHOICE

In April, a strapping defensive lineman named Richard Seymour had been the team's first draft choice, despite the fact that many people believed what they needed most were deep-threat pass receivers for Bledsoe. Coach Bill Belichick insisted Seymour would make a bigger impact, but within days the unraveling of Glenn went into motion, and it seemed even clearer that a major need had not been addressed.

Before the season's first game was played, Glenn was arrested on a domestic assault charge after an argument with his former girlfriend, was suspended by the NFL for four games for violating the league's substance abuse policy, was suspended for the season by the Patriots after storming out of training camp when he learned owner Bob Kraft would attempt to withhold more than $8 million in bonus money due him and try to recoup the portion he had already paid him for violating behavioral clauses in his contract, and filed an appeal of the team's suspension that he would eventually win.

If that wasn't bad enough, the offensive line saw one player after another go down with preseason injuries, including second-round choice

Though not by choice, Drew Bledsoe had a hand in Tom Brady's elevation to starter, and the Patriots' climb into the NFL elite.

Matt Light, who had been projected to be the starting left tackle, guards Joe Andruzzi and Mike Compton, and center Damien Woody. Guard Joe Panos, who along with Compton was a key offseason free-agent addition, decided he'd seen enough after the conditioning run and retired one day into his tenure as a Patriot starter. And so the summer went.

It was one thing after another, it seemed. Defensive end Willie McGinest had his back surgically repaired in June, and although the team tried to downplay it at the time by calling it a "surgical procedure" rather than surgery, McGinest would be limited all season by pain and stiffness and seldom looked like himself.

Then came one of the cruelest blows when 45-year-old quarterbacks coach Dick Rehbein died unexpectedly of a heart condition in early August. It seemed nothing was going to go right, and that feeling did not improve when the season opened in Cincinnati with 11 new starters. It was a familiar result. The Bengals tore through New England's defense for 157 rushing yards and sacked Bledsoe four times on the way to a 23-17 victory.

CONTROVERSY BREWING

Bad as it seemed that day, the game was quickly forgotten as the events of Sept. 11 overshadowed anything going on in Foxborough. When the NFL returned Sept. 23, it was a highly emotional day because Andruzzi's three brothers, New York City firemen who had been working at the World Trade Center, stood by his side. One had nearly been trapped in the collapsing towers and when the 300-pound Andruzzi told their story, he broke into tears. So did anyone who listened.

That Sunday the Andruzzi family was honored before the game and stood at midfield for the opening coin toss of what would prove to be a season-turning four quarters. The Patriots lost the game and Bledsoe that day, the former because of four turnovers that included two fumbles inside the 20-yard line and the latter from injuries so severe that there were major concerns about the blood loss Bledsoe suffered in the first hours after Lewis leveled him.

Now 0-2 and facing the undefeated and high-flying Indianapolis Colts with an untested quarterback and a team questioning itself, trouble seemed to have the Patriots surrounded. But linebacker Bryan Cox, who had become one of the team's spiritual leaders in his first days in New England, said simply, "They ain't going to cancel the season." His attitude was "press on" and so they did, rallying behind him and other veterans like Roman Phifer, Anthony Pleasant, and the always reliable Troy Brown.

Instead of canceling the season, the Patriots canceled out Peyton Manning and the Colts once again. With Tom Brady operating efficiently and Antowain Smith running free for the first time, New England dominated, beating Indianapolis and Manning for the fourth straight time, 44-13, by intercepting three passes and returning two for touchdowns while they shut down an offense that had been averaging 43.5 points a game by keeping them off the scoreboard until only 0:53 remained in the third quarter.

"We aren't a bad team," Cox insisted. "Sometimes we lack confidence but we're a good team."

When the Dolphins' defense took them and Brady apart (86 yards passing, four sacks) the next Sunday to drop them to 1-3, they did not look like a good team, but they bounced back with a huge overtime win in Foxborough over Doug Flutie's Chargers the next weekend on a day when Brady threw for 364 yards and two touchdowns and Glenn returned from suspension to catch seven passes for 110 yards and a score. Now a quarterback controversy was brewing as Bledsoe slowly worked his way back to health, and people began to ask when he would be back under center.

ON THE COMEBACK TRAIL

Brady quelled such talk quickly by beating the Colts again a week later, 38-17, but the big story that day was little David Patten, whom Belichick had brought in as a free agent. The receiver notched the football hat trick, scoring on a 29-yard run, receptions of 91 and 6 yards, and by tossing a perfect 60-yard scoring pass to Brown. The Colts had no answers.

But a week later in Denver, Brady came crashing down to earth again. After throwing an NFL-record 162 passes without an interception to open his career, Brady was intercepted four times in the fourth quarter of a 31-20 loss to the Broncos that unsettled people who kept waiting for the absence of Bledsoe to deal a death blow to the Patriots.

But Brady's steadiness under pressure, the emergence of Smith as a 1,000-yard running back threat, and a relentless and tricky defense coordinated by often brilliant Romeo Crennel prevented it. New England won eight of its next nine games to go from 3-4 and a team on the ropes to one of the unlikeliest division champions in league history.

Along the way, it would lose Cox to a broken leg, and two defensive fixtures of the past, McGinest and Ted Johnson, would seldom be seen. Same was true of Glenn, who never made his presence felt after the San Diego game except in those odd moments when his absence made headlines.

Led by a quarterback with no experience, a running back no one wanted, and a defense of no-names with the exception of Lawyer Milloy and Ty Law, the Patriots rolled through the second half of the season, defeating Atlanta, Buffalo twice, New Orleans, the Jets, Cleveland, and Miami before locking up the division title and a first-round bye in the playoffs by battering the

Carolina Panthers, 38-6, on a day in which they played, by their own admission, sloppily.

While the 1-14 Panthers were admittedly among the worst teams in the NFL, the Patriots of three months ago seemed unlikely to have been able to beat anyone on a day when they would turn the ball over four times. But by now they had become a clever offensive team manipulated by the mind of offensive coordinator Charlie Weis and a resourceful defensive one that on this day would return two interceptions for touchdowns and have a third called back, while Brown returned his second punt in a month for a touchdown when he slithered and sped 68 yards through the broken Panthers' special teams.

Thus ended a stunning rise from nowhere to somewhere by a team few had expected much of before the season began, and even fewer thought about after Bledsoe was knocked out for what turned out to be the year. After seven weeks of rehabilitation, Bledsoe was finally ready to return, but by then Brady was on his way to going 11-3 as a starter and leaving Belichick no choice but to maintain the status quo.

That Bledsoe felt he had been promised a chance to compete for what he still called "my job" when he was healthy again was obvious. When it didn't come he was stunned and angry, yet he bit his lip — as Cox would do later under similar circumstances when Tedy Bruschi took over at middle linebacker — and continued to support Brady on the sideline while Brady became his peers' choice as one of three AFC Pro Bowl quarterbacks.

It was a remarkable end to a story that seemed to have no chance of a happy conclusion. Not even Glenn's continued problems could alter this Cinderella fable as the playoffs approached. ⊘

Turning point

The ball was down, but not out. The Patriots would continue their improbable run, through the snow and the Steel Curtain, ultimately closing down The Greatest Show on Turf.

Raiders

Vinatieri knocks Raiders out cold

16-13

OAK	0	7	6	0	0
NE	0	0	3	10	3

FOXBOROUGH
In an incredible comeback, sparked by an incredibly controversial call by referee Walt Coleman, the Patriots were headed for the AFC championship game following a 16-13 overtime victory over the Oakland Raiders on Adam Vinatieri's 23-yard field goal into the wind and a heavy snow at Foxboro Stadium.

The Patriots drove 61 yards after winning the toss and receiving the ball in OT.

Quarterback Tom Brady, who had

On a nip-and-tuck play ultimately ruled an incompletion, Tom Brady loses the ball.

looked overmatched for much of the game, drove the Patriots into field goal territory twice late, once for Vinatieri to tie it with 27 seconds left in regulation from 45 yards on a low, line-drive kick. Then he got the Patriots close enough for Vinatieri to win the game.

"I line-drived it and then I had to wait a second to see if it was going to go over," said Vinatieri of his tying field

TO TIE

Adam Vinatieri punched a low, line-drive kick 45 yards through the wind and snow to tie the game with 27 seconds left...

TO WIN

then he sent the Patriots on to Pittsburgh with a 23-yarder in overtime. Ken Walter provided the spot both times.

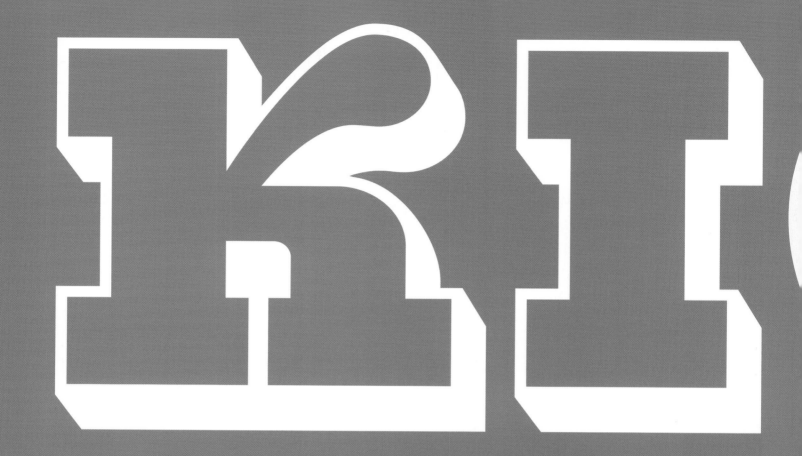

2001

Adam Vinatieri's 48-yard field goal in the Super Bowl started the team's meteoric rise.

2003

Ken Walter had 25 punts downed inside the opponent's 20-yard line, and just 3 touchbacks.

POSTSEASON Vinatieri is second all-time in field goals made in

2004

Vinatieri was successful on a career-high
31 of his 33 field-goal attempts
and scored a career-high 141 points.

the postseason with 24, second only to Gary Anderson's 32.

goal. "On the game-winner, I knew we had to get it down. I knew we were close-in range. During the timeout, we cleared off some snow, and we did it on third down just in case something happened."

The Patriots' defense made two key stops in the fourth quarter, and then got the ball back with 2:06 remaining after Troy Brown's punt return of 27 yards to the 46. He fumbled, but the Patriots recovered.

Helped by the two-minute warning, the Patriots had no timeouts left, and the ball was on the 42.

Then they were saved by the controversial call.

Charles Woodson came in untouched on a corner blitz from the left side, and appeared to force Brady to fumble on first and 10. It seemed Brady had tucked the ball, which after the hit was recovered by linebacker Greg Biekert on the Oakland 48.

The officials reviewed the play and Coleman came back and ruled that Brady was going forward with his arm.

"His arm was going forward and the call was made. It was out of our hands," said Patriots coach Bill Belichick.

According to Coleman, "Obviously, what I saw on the field, I thought the ball came out before his arm was going forward. Then, when I got to the replay monitor and looked at it, it was obvious his arm was coming forward. He touched the ball. And they just hooked it out of his hand. His arm was coming forward, which makes it an incomplete pass."

Oakland coach Jon Gruden didn't see it that way. "In my opinion it was a fumble, but obviously I don't understand [the rule]. But I thought it was a fumble," said Gruden.

Brady said, "Yeah, I was throwing the ball."

Many Patriots fans could only think it was revenge for a disputed roughing-the-passer penalty in the teams' 1976 playoff game.

The Patriots moved to the Oakland 28, but finally opted to kick.

"We didn't have any choice. We had a lot of confidence in Adam to make it," said Belichick. "You have to give a lot of credit to [long-snapper] Lonie [Paxton] and Kenny [Walter] for the hold. They were tough conditions."

"Tom did a nice job in the no-huddle offense there in the end," said Belichick. "The receivers made some good catches in those conditions. At this time you have to be at the highest in concentration and alertness, and they were."

Brady completed eight straight passes, four to Jermaine Wiggins (who had 10 catches), three to David Patten, and one to Kevin Faulk before Brady scrambled in from the 6 with 7:52 remaining to pull to within 13-10.

Belichick said he and his staff watched tapes of the Buffalo blizzard game in 2000, and at the last minute included plays that were successful in that game. Wiggins caught a couple of big balls in that game.

"Jermaine had a couple of big catches in that game. He's kind of a snow plow for us," said Belichick.

Vinatieri hit from 23 yards out with 8:39 remaining in the third quarter, but even more impressive was Sebastian Janikowski's 38-yarder with 4:14 remaining in the third to make it 10-3.

"As the game went along, the range kind of dwindled down a little," said Vinatieri.

After an awful first half, the Patriots took the opening kickoff in the second half, and moved the ball well.

Brady connected on two long passes to Patten, one for 25 yards and the other for 19 to the Raiders 9. But Brady overthrew Patten and Rod Rutledge in

the end zone, forcing Vinatieri to boot a field goal, making it 7-3.

The Raiders did not seem deterred. The next possession saw Rich Gannon complete medium-range passes of 15, 10, and 10 yards to Tim Brown, Jerry Rice, and James Jett. The Raiders got it to the 21 before Janikowski made his first of two big second-half field goals.

After the Patriots went three and out on their next series, the Raiders again got close for Janikowski. The big play was a 22-yard pass from Gannon to Rice. After his team advanced to the Patriots' 27, Janikowski hit from 45 yards to make it a 13-3 game with 1:41 remaining in the third.

Both teams struggled with the weather, but early in the second quarter, the Raiders got a break on a special teams mistake by Je'Rod Cherry, who interfered with a fair catch attempt by Woodson.

The 15-yard penalty allowed the Raiders to start their drive at midfield.

Gannon, 10 for 14 for 87 yards in the first half, certainly appeared to be much more nimble in the snow at that point than Brady. He went right to work, connecting with Charlie Garner for a 12-yard play to the New England 38. Gannon had a lot of time to throw, and he sat in the pocket and completed a 10-yard pass to Jeremy Brigham to the 27.

On third and 8, Gannon connected on a slant to Rice to the 13. Two plays later, Gannon sent a fade to the end zone for Jett, who beat Terrance Shaw and caught the ball untouched for 6 points.

Janikowski added the extra point to give the Raiders a 7-0 lead with 12:14 remaining in the second.

But that was a part of the game that few will remember. They'll only remember the Call, the snow, and the kicks. ✐

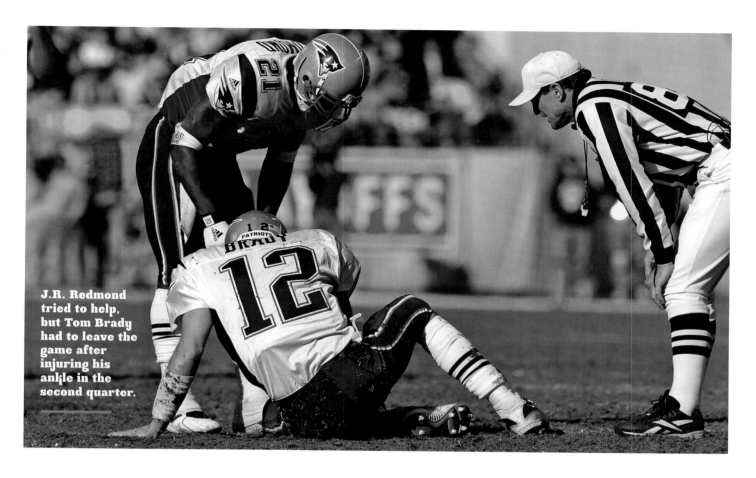

J.R. Redmond tried to help, but Tom Brady had to leave the game after injuring his ankle in the second quarter.

Steelers

Respect, revenge and a title, too

24-17

NE	7	7	7	3
PIT	0	3	14	0

PITTSBURGH

Quarterback Drew Bledsoe hoisted the AFC Championship trophy and pumped it three times on the podium as teammates, owner Robert Kraft, and coach Bill Belichick waved, pumped their fists, and soaked in an improbable moment in an improbable season.

Players were hollering and screaming with joy and happiness. Feelings of accomplishment, and some of revenge, flowed like the champagne that was tactfully absent as the Patriots celebrated a 24-17 victory over the Pittsburgh Steelers at Heinz Field, putting them into Super Bowl XXXVI in New Orleans.

In the end, safety Lawyer Milloy, one of several players who want to complete unfinished business from the Super Bowl in New Orleans after the 1996 season, got his respect from the perhaps-overconfident Steelers.

Belichick got to the Super Bowl with the Patriots again, this time as the head coach, not a Bill Parcells underling.

Bledsoe, who entered the game in the second quarter in relief of Tom Brady (injured ankle) and led the team to a quick score and eventually a victory, just stood crying. The tears were flowing freely, and when he caught a glimpse of his father, Mac, he lost it completely.

From Bledsoe suffering a life-threatening hit by the Jets' Mo Lewis, to losing his job to Brady when he was ready to play, to returning after four months of inactivity to direct the Patriots in the AFC title game?

Quite a fairy tale, folks.

"You never disrespect anybody," said Milloy, who chastised the Steelers at a press conference Friday for talking about Super Bowl plans and overlooking the Patriots.

"You just make it hard on yourself. I'm just surprised the veterans on that team didn't shut the younger guys' mouths," Milloy said. "It was a momentum-builder for us. We rallied around that, and in the end we were the AFC champions."

Kraft said he congratulated his

who knew he had to make a big play and got a nice block by Tedy Bruschi. "It was just a great play by the punt-return team."

Just before the punt return, Brown's third for a touchdown this season, Miller had lofted a 64-yarder that Brown opted not to field and allowed to scoot past him to the 23. But Steelers special-teamer Troy Edwards was called for running out of bounds,

sprained his ankle when Lee Flowers crawled over somebody and rolled into the back of his legs. No penalty was called.

Bledsoe entered with 1:40 remaining in the first half and hit David Patten on a 15-yard pass to the Steeler 25 for a first down. He was forced to run for 4 yards, and Chad Scott's big sideline hit, knocking Bledsoe way out of bounds, looked eerily like the Lewis blast in the second game of the season. The officials did not throw a flag, because even though Scott left his feet, Bledsoe was not yet out of bounds when he was crunched.

Bledsoe, who cut his chin on the play, got right back up, and appeared fired-up. He found Patten for 10 yards to the 11, and then threw a beauty of a TD pass to Patten in the right corner of the end zone with 58 seconds remaining.

His play after all that time off was nothing short of extraordinary.

"He gets very few reps," said offensive coordinator Charlie Weis. "I'd say he should be proud. That's a pretty hard thing we asked him to do."

It was 14-3 at the half, and who could have scripted it? Belichick was asked if Brady could have continued.

"He could have gone back out and played, but I just felt like the way things were going we were better at that point in time [with Bledsoe]," the coach said. "We were better with a healthy Drew Bledsoe with not knowing where Tom was with his injury."

Stewart drove the Steelers to the Patriots 16 in the third quarter, but they had to settle for a field-goal attempt. Brown, who had been shaky all season, had a 34-yard attempt, but Brandon Mitchell fought through his blocks and came in with his hands up, deflecting the ball. Troy Brown, the epitome of Belichick's "Be Alert" mantra during the week, picked up the

Drew Bledsoe, New England's signature player for nearly a decade, came off the bench to help win the AFC Championship.

team on a great season.

"This is the true meaning of team," said Kraft. "We never talk about individuals here."

He did say of Belichick, "[He] was worth everything we gave up to get him two years ago."

The message was sent early — at the coin toss, in fact — when the Steelers' Jerome Bettis started to talk trash. Bryan Cox, a Patriots defensive co-captain, got in his face immediately.

"I just wanted to make a point that we were not backing down," Cox said. "He started talking about how he was ready and all this and that, and I said, 'Jerome, this ain't what you're gonna be looking for today.'"

When Josh Miller banged a 47-yard punt late in the first quarter, the Patriots' Troy Brown fielded it and raced up the middle, going 55 yards for a touchdown. Adam Vinatieri's extra point made it 7-0 with 3:42 remaining in the first. "It was supposed to be a left return, but the guys overplayed it to the outside, and I saw the seam up the middle and we just hit it," said Brown,

and the officials forced another punt.

Terrell Buckley had chased Edwards down the sideline, perhaps causing him to step out of bounds.

"It's not something I did by design, but if I can crowd him and make him go out, that's a legitimate call," said Buckley. "We got the re-punt and Troy did the rest."

On the Steelers' second play after Brown's punt return, Kordell Stewart got loose for a 34-yard gain after hurdling Milloy in the backfield. That got the ball to the New England 38. Four plays later, he had the Steelers first and 10 at the Patriots 13. But New England's tough red-zone defense stiffened, as Anthony Pleasant sacked Stewart for a 2-yard loss and good coverage by Otis Smith on Plaxico Burress resulted in an incompletion, forcing the Steelers to settle for a 30-yard field goal by Kris Brown.

Brady completed 12 of 18 passes for 115 yards before leaving the game. He faced constant pressure from linebacker Jason Gildon, who was all over the field. Late in the first half, Brady

Drew Bledsoe helped win the AFC championship trophy, and also won some redemption with his play vs. Pittsburgh.

loose ball and ran 11 yards before lateraling to safety Antwan Harris. He went the remaining 49 yards for the score, giving the Patriots a 21-3 lead.

"I saw Antwan coming, over my shoulder, and he was screaming my name," said Brown. "From there, I just wanted to make sure it was a lateral, and he did a great job. It worked out great for us."

Mitchell was screaming and laughing all the way down the field.

"I had so much fun out there," the lineman said. But the game was far from over.

With Bettis ineffective (8 yards on 9 carries), Stewart took to the air. He found The Bus on an 11-yard hookup, then connected with Hines Ward for 24. That turned into an eight-play, 79-yard drive capped by Bettis's 1-yard run with 5:11 remaining in the third quarter, to make it 21-10.

A momentum shift was in progress. On the next series, the Pittsburgh defense toughened. J.R. Redmond dropped a pass and Bledsoe was sacked by Gildon during a three-and-out series.

The Steelers got a 28-yard return on a 38-yard punt by Ken Walter to the New England 32. It took five plays and an 11-yard run by Amos Zereoue to make this a too-close 21-17 game late in the third.

Vinatieri nailed a 44-yard field goal early in the fourth, creating a 7-point advantage. Linebacker Joey Porter missed a Bledsoe pass thrown right to him, when he could have walked in for a touchdown, midway through the fourth.

A huge Tebucky Jones interception of Stewart foiled another Steelers attempt late in the game.

Vinatieri missed a 50-yarder to the left with 2:21 left, but the Patriots held on, compiling the first eight-game win streak in team history. ⌀

ANKLE, HIS STATUS UNCERTAIN FOR SUPER BOWL; NEW ENGLAND HEADS TO ITS 3RD SUPER BOWL, ALL IN NEW ORLEANS

Champions!

BY DAN SHAUGHNESSY

Rams

Patriots are superheroes

20-17

NE	0	14	3	3
STL	3	0	0	14

NEW ORLEANS
This time, the ball didn't scoot between anyone's legs. It sailed between the uprights. Straight and true.

This time, there was no ill-timed penalty for too many players on the field. No black cloud. No bad calls. No Charlie Brown luck.

Adam Vinatieri's last-second, 48-yard field goal dropped over the crossbar and gave the New England Patriots a 20-17 victory over the St. Louis Rams in what may have been the greatest Super Bowl of them all. Under the Superdome's synthetic sky, 1,500 miles from home, the Patriots

shocked the nation and delivered Greater Boston its first professional sports championship since 1986.

On his way to becoming a Bobby Orr/Larry Bird of the new century, Kid Tom Brady produced one final miracle to complete the magic ride of 2001-02. The wonderboy quarterback concluded his stardust season by copping the MVP and becoming the youngest winning QB (24) in Super Bowl history.

"The way we felt was that we were the better team," he said. "Absolutely incredible. It's what happens when guys believe in each other. And there's so many reasons why we're here."

Brady was hardly dominant (16 for 27, 145 yards, one touchdown, no interceptions), but after St. Louis tied the game at 17 with 1:30 left, he drove the Patriots 53 yards in eight plays (without benefit of timeouts), putting Vinatieri in position to win the game.

So after four quarters of bone-rattling, blood-and-thunder defense, the Pats won it on a walk-off kick by the kid from South Dakota. And for

the second time in three weeks, long snapper Lonie Paxton celebrated on his back with traditional snow angels amid the confetti of the end zone.

While more confetti fluttered from the ceiling, Patriots owner Bob Kraft accepted the Vince Lombardi Trophy from commissioner Paul Tagliabue and said, "The fans of New England have been waiting 42 years. We are the world champions. At this time in our country, we are all Patriots, and tonight the Patriots are champions."

These Patriots seemed to thrive in their position as underdogs. A last-place team one year ago, listed at 75-1 to win the Super Bowl before the season, they jelled under the leadership of coach Bill Belichick and the quarterbacking of Brady. They won their final nine games, and this shocker ranks as the second-greatest upset in Super Bowl history (the Rams were favored by 14), exceeded only by Joe Namath's 18-point underdog Jets in 1969.

New England suffocated St. Louis's high-flying offense, holding the Rams

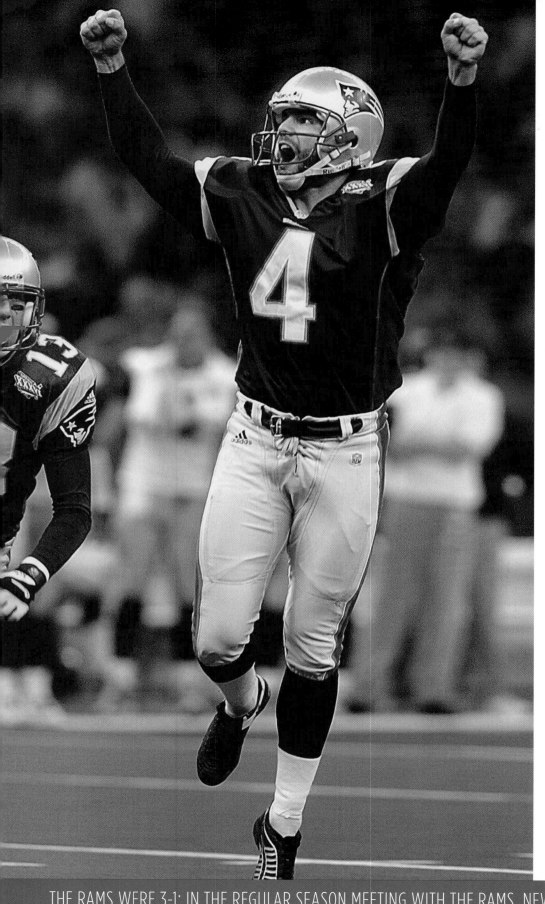

In a suspended moment that lasted no more than a second or two, Vinatieri's arms were raised and the Patriots on the sideline crashed onto the Superdome turf, displaying some of the most intense and heartfelt emotion ever seen in the sport.

Rams receiver Torry Holt got an early taste of the Patriots' defensive recipe, as he was sandwiched between Tebucky Jones and Tedy Bruschi.

to 3 points over the first three quarters and forcing three turnovers. The fumble and two picks led to all of the Pats' 17 points up to then. The Rams averaged 31 points and didn't score fewer than 15 in any game all season.

"It was force vs. finesse and something had to give," said Patriot linebacker Tedy Bruschi.

New England's ferocious defense hurried and hurt the Rams for 3½ quarters. Warner's only touchdown pass in the first three quarters was thrown to Patriots cornerback Ty Law.

The second St. Louis turnover came with just under a minute and a half to go in the second quarter. Ricky Proehl caught a pass over the middle and was rocked by Antwan Harris. The ball came loose and was scooped up by New England's Terrell Buckley, who ran it to the Ram 40.

While the stunned Ram offense tried to regroup, Brady went to work. With 31 seconds left in the half, he connected with David Patten on a timing route in the corner of the end zone. Patten's circus catch sent the underdogs into halftime with a 14-3 lead.

The Rams hadn't trailed by more than 8 points all year. No Super Bowl team had ever overcome a halftime deficit of more than 7 points.

New England's defense was even better in the third period, and the Rams were rattled. Patriots cornerback Otis Smith picked off a pass when wideout Torry Holt fell down, and that led to a 37-yard field goal by Vinatieri and a 17-3 Patriot lead.

Then came some anxious moments for Patriot Nation. On a fourth-and-goal from the 3, Warner was hit by Roman Phifer and fumbled. The ball was picked up by Tebucky Jones, who ran the length of the field for a touchdown.

No. Penalty.

Patriots veteran Willie McGinest

David Patten snagged a high spiral from Tom Brady and gracefully tumbled into the end zone for a second-quarter touchdown.

was caught holding Marshall Faulk, and the TD came back. Warner eventually scored on a quarterback keeper.

Instead of leading, 24-3, with 10:09 left, the Pats led, 17-10, with 9:31 left.

Snake-bitten New Englanders fretted. Would "McGinest held the

tailback" succeed "Pesky held the ball" in our local sports Hall of Pain?

It sure looked that way when the Rams tied the game on a three-play, 55-yard touchdown drive. At best, it appeared Super Bowl XXXVI would be the first to go into overtime.

But Brady had one more miracle in his bag. He took over on his own 17 with 1:21 left and no timeouts. And he did the job. The key play was a 23-yard pass to Troy Brown. A short pass to Jermaine Wiggins put the ball on the 30 and set the stage for Vinatieri.

"I was just so happy that the guys moved the ball down and gave me an opportunity," said Vinatieri. "Once I kicked it, I knew it was good. I looked up and it was just time to celebrate. It was unbelievable."

In the winners' locker room, a couple of Wheaties boxes surfaced - boxes with the images of Brady and four of his teammates. Brady signed one for Troy Brown, then went back out to the field to do some more interviews.

"Beat those Red Sox, huh?" Kid Brady said with a grin.

So there. The drought is over. The Patriots will be defending Super Bowl champs when they first play in their brand new stadium next fall. The oft-maligned football team from Foxborough has empowered us with bragging rights across the land.

These Patriots did something no Red Sox team has done in 83 years, something no Bruins team has done in 30 years, and something no Celtic team has achieved since Larry and Friends beat the Rockets in '86.

Hold your heads high, New England sports fans. No matter whether you live in Boston, Foxborough, Hartford, or Groton, you woke up this morning in a city of champions.

Open the fridge and pull out that bottle of bubbly that's been chilling for 16 long years. ✏

WINNERS

David Patten kicked up his heels, and Tedy Bruschi planted a kiss on football's ultimate prize.

SALARY OF $298,000; IT IS THE ONLY SUPER BOWL TO BE DECIDED BY A LAST-SECOND FIELD GOAL.

Glad all over

New England sports fans uncorked their passions on the frigid streets of Boston in a red-white-and-blue explosion of championship joy. From Copley Square to City Hall Plaza, a crowd estimated at 1.25 million, twice the population of Boston, cheered the world champions.

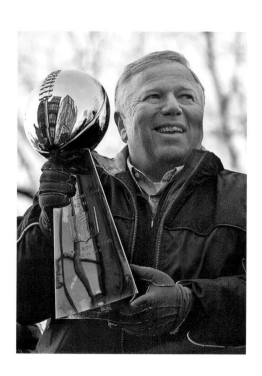

PARADE ROOT

Lawyer Milloy said, "Here it is, y'all!" after the hard hats entertained the crowd by spelling out P-A-T-S. Owner Robert Kraft and coach Bill Belichick and family returned the fans' salutes.

2001 ROSTER

#	NAME	POS	HT	WT	AGE	YR	WHEN/HOW ACQUIRED	COLLEGE
4	Adam Vinatieri	K	6'0"	200	29	6	1996 free agent	South Dakota State
11	Drew Bledsoe	QB	6'5"	240	29	9	1993 Draft—1st Round	Washington State
12	Tom Brady	QB	6'4"	220	24	2	2000 Draft—6th Round	Michigan
13	Ken Walter	P	6'1"	195	29	4	2001 free agent	Kent State
15	Jimmy Farris	WR	6'0"	200	23	R	2002 Rookie free agent	Montana
19	Damon Huard	QB	6'3"	220	28	5	2001 free agent (MIA)	Washington
21	J.R. Redmond	RB	5'11"	215	24	2	2000 Draft—3rd Round	Arizona State
22	Terrance Shaw	CB	5'11"	200	28	7	2001 free agent	Stephen F. Austin
23	Antwan Harris	CB	5'9"	192	24	2	2000 Draft—6th Round	Virginia
24	Ty Law	CB	5'11"	199	27	7	1995 Draft—1st Round	Michigan
25	Leonard Myers	CB	5'10"	195	23	R	2001 Draft—6th Round	Miami
27	Terrell Buckley	CB	5'9"	176	30	10	2001 free agent	Florida State
30	Je'Rod Cherry	DB	6'1"	205	28	6	2001 free agent	California
32	Antowain Smith	RB	6'2"	230	29	5	2001 free agent	Houston
33	Kevin Faulk	RB	5'8"	202	25	3	1999 Draft—2nd Round	Louisiana State
34	Tebucky Jones	FS	6'2"	218	27	4	1998 Draft—1st Round	Syracuse
35	Patrick Pass	FB	5'10"	217	24	2	2000 Draft—7th Round	Georgia
36	Lawyer Milloy	SS	6'0"	207	28	6	1996 Draft—2nd Round	Washington
44	Marc Edwards	FB	6'0"	245	27	5	2001 free agent	Notre Dame
45	Otis Smith	CB	5'11"	196	36	12	2000 free agent	Missouri
48	Arther Love	TE	6'4"	250	24	R	2001 Draft—6th Round	South Carolina State
50	Mike Vrabel	LB	6'4"	250	26	5	2001 free agent (PIT)	Ohio State
51	Brian Cox	LB	6'4"	250	33	10	2001 free agent (NYJ)	Western Illinois
52	Ted Johnson	LB	6'4"	253	29	7	1995 Draft—2nd Round	Colorado
53	Larry Izzo	LB	5'10"	228	27	6	2001 free agent (MIA)	Rice
54	Tedy Bruschi	LB	6'1"	247	28	6	1996 Draft—3rd Round	Arizona
55	Willie McGinest	DE	6'5"	270	30	8	1994 Draft-1st Round	Southern California
58	Matt Chatham	LB	6'4"	250	24	2	2000 Waivers (STL)	South Dakota
61	Stephen Neal	DT	6'2"	290	25	R	2001 Rookie free agent	Cal State Bakersfield
63	Joe Andruzzi	G	6'3"	315	26	5	2000 free agent	Southern Connecticut St.
64	Greg Robinson-Randall	T	6'5"	322	23	2	2000 Draft—4th Round	Michigan State
65	Damien Woody	C	6'3"	320	24	3	1999 Draft—1st Round	Boston College
66	Lonie Paxton	LS	6'2"	260	23	2	2000 Rookie free agent	Sacramento State
67	Greg Ruegamer	C/G	6'5"	322	25	3	2000 Rookie free agent	Arizona State
71	Chris Sullivan	DE	6'4"	285	28	6	2001 free agent	Boston College
72	Matt Light	T	6'4"	305	23	R	2001 Draft—2nd Round	Purdue
76	Kenyatta Jones	T	6'3"	305	23	R	2001 Draft—4th Round	South Florida
76	Grant Williams	T	6'7"	320	27	6	2000 free agent	Louisiana Tech

#	NAME	POS	HT	WT	AGE	YR	WHEN/HOW ACQUIRED	COLLEGE
77	Mike Compton	G/C	6'6"	310	31	9	2001 free agent	West Virginia
80	Troy Brown	WR	5'10"	193	30	9	1993 Draft—8th Round	Marshall
81	Charles Johnson	WR	6'10"	205	30	8	2001 free agent	Colorado
83	Rod Rutledge	TE	6'5"	265	26	4	1998 Draft—2nd Round	Alabama
84	Fred Coleman	WR	6'0"	190	27	1	2001 Rookie free agent	Washington
85	Jermaine Wiggins	TE	6'2"	255	27	2	2000 Waivers	Georgia
86	**David Patten**	**WR**	**5'10"**	**190**	**27**	**5**	**2001 free agent (CLE)**	**Western Carolina**
91	Bobby Hamilton	DE	6'5"	280	31	7	2000 free agent (NYJ)	Southern Mississippi
92	David Nugent	DL	6'4"	295	24	2	2000 Draft—6th Round	Purdue
93	Richard Seymour	DL	6'6"	305	22	R	2001 Draft—1st Round	Georgia
94	Ty Warren	DL	6'5"	300	22	R	2003 Draft—1st Round	Texas A&M
95	Roman Phifer	LB	6'2"	240	33	11	2001 free agent (NYJ)	UCLA
96	Brandon Mitchell	DL	6'3"	280	26	5	1997 Draft—2nd Round	Texas A&M
97	Riddick Parker	DL	6'3"	295	29	5	2001 free agent	North Carolina
98	Anthony Pleasant	DE	6'5"	280	34	12	2001 free agent (SF)	Tennessee State

COACHES

HEAD COACH Bill Belichick

ASSISTANTS: DEFENSIVE COORDINATOR & DEFENSIVE LINE Romeo Crennel
ASSISTANT OFFENSIVE LINE Jeff Davidson / WIDE RECEIVERS Ivan Fears /
QUARTERBACKS John Hufnagel / INSIDE LINEBACKERS Pepper Johnson
DEFENSIVE BACKS Eric Mangini / COACHING ASSISTANT Josh McDaniels
DEFENSIVE LINE Randy Melvin / ASSISTANT STRENGTH & CONDITIONING Markus Paul
OUTSIDE LINEBACKERS Rob Ryan / ASSISTANT HEAD COACH & OFFENSIVE LINE
Dante Scarnecchia / SPECIAL TEAMS Brad Seely
OFFENSIVE COORDINATOR & RUNNING BACKS Charlie Weis

> "You just try to take the situation at hand and do the best you can with it. When it is over, recalibrate, reload, and go again. We never sit there and think, 'Well, if this happens, where are we going to be two months from now?' We just never look at it like that."
>
> *— Bill Belichick*

ONCE MORE, WITH FEELING

CHAPTER TWO

2003 predictions

10-6

They could be the class of the AFC East if Ted Washington holds up and their Flying Wallenda offense stays more balanced than a year ago. **RON BORGES**

10-6

Winning 10 games in this division is quite a feat. Expect one of the other teams to match (the bet here is Miami), but the Patriots should make the playoffs as a wild card. **NICK CAFARDO**

11-5

Will be AFC champions. Milloy chat will cease by Week 4 as defense stands tall and Brady silences doubters — and you know who you are — with quality QB-ing. **BOB RYAN**

10-6

New England gets the best wild card in football and baseball.
DAN SHAUGHNESSY

8-8

Can't run. Can't stop run. No playoff run. **MICHAEL SMITH**

FINAL  14-2

Regular Season

Buffalo Bills
Philadelphia Eagles
New York Jets
Washington Redskins
Tennessee Titans
New York Giants
Miami Dolphins
Cleveland Browns
Denver Broncos
Dallas Cowboys
Houston Texans
Indianapolis Colts
Miami Dolphins
Jacksonville Jaguars
New York Jets
Buffalo Bills

Postseason

Tennessee Titans
Indianapolis Colts
Carolina Panthers

03

Bills
Topsy-turvy start to season

0 - 31

NE	0	0	0	0
BUF	7	14	0	10

BUFFALO

It was as if the Bills were the Patriots and the Patriots were the Bills. It was as if Tom Brady was Drew Bledsoe, and vice versa. It was Buffalo coach Gregg Williams being asked whether he had gotten into Brady's head, with nobody wondering if the Patriots' Bill Belichick had gotten into Bledsoe's head, as is often the case.

After 2002's two lopsided Patriots wins, one might have expected a downtrodden Buffalo team and an upbeat New England squad, and a Patriots victory. What happened, a 31-0 Buffalo win, the worst opening-day loss in Patriots' history, was just the opposite.

Five days after Lawyer Milloy's release from the Patriots over a contract dispute, he was still on the winning side of a game the Bills could not have orchestrated any better. Milloy, who started at strong safety, made five tackles and was credited with an 11-yard sack of Brady. He made a key play by defending a pass in the back of the end zone intended for David Patten, enabling Nate Clements to grab the deflection for an interception.

The last starter introduced, Milloy came out with a new dance that he had especially designed for his new fans in Buffalo.

"I don't think the Bills needed Lawyer to get them going," said Patri-ots guard Mike Compton. "The rest of their guys outplayed us in every phase of the game."

Conversely, the Patriots were flat from the outset.

If there was one other undeniable observation about the Bills, it was that their revamped defense seems like it may be special. At least it was on this warm day before 73,262 at Ralph Wilson Stadium. To shut out the Patriots, who were last blanked Nov. 8, 1993, by the Jets, 6-0, was overwhelming evidence. Newcomers Takeo Spikes and Sam Adams were big differences on a defense that ran over the Patriots, limiting Brady to a 14-for-29 effort for 123 yards and four interceptions, clearly his worst as a Patriot.

"There was nothing good that came out of that game," said Brady. "It's the first time we've faced adversity in six weeks and we've got to rebound. From the opening kickoff to the last play of the game, it was all one-sided."

Adams sealed the game when he picked off Brady with 10:24 remaining in the second quarter. The big man rambled 37 yards down the right sideline, carrying the pigskin like Ricky Williams but doing this "40" in perhaps the slowest time in NFL history. Yet blocks by London Fletcher and Aaron Schobel kept him protected, making it 21-0.

"Our defense," said an ecstatic Bledsoe, "Jeez. They were tremendous out there."

Bledsoe, who was 17 for 28 for 230 yards, with one touchdown and one interception, wasn't bad either. When Bledsoe can play with a lead, not force balls into coverage, and use his running game, it's usually going to be a long day for the opposition.

Another ex-Patriot, Sam Gash, opened up good holes as a lead blocker for Travis Henry, who ran 28 times for 86 yards.

Eagles
Struggles are quickly forgotten

31 - 10

NE	3	14	7	7
PHI	0	7	0	3

PHILADELPHIA

After a long seven days of postmortems following the worst passing performance of his career in a season-opening 31-0 loss to the Buffalo branch of the Patriots, Tom Brady came back at Lincoln Financial Field as if it was still 2001.

He was accurate, not antsy. He was productive, not passive. He was patient, not petulant. He was, in other words, Tom Brady, and the result was not only a 31-10 victory over the Philadelphia Eagles, but an afternoon in which he finished 30 for 44 for 255 passing yards and three touchdowns. His quarterback rating was 105.8, his highest since the Kansas City game in 2002, in which he passed for 410 yards and four touchdowns.

The difference between those two games a year apart was that last season Brady was still The Golden Boy with the Super Bowl MVP under his arm. After last week's terrible defeat, in which he threw four interceptions and finished with an abysmal 22.5 quarterback rating, that award and a lot of other things about his game had been forgotten. Suddenly there were more questions than answers about Brady and the offense he ran and Charlie Weis designed, because it had struggled in the final month last season and seemed to be beginning a new year still on its knees.

Christian Fauria was alive and kicking with two TD catches against the Eagles.

season, and those throws made the score 17-7. From that point on, the Eagles were reeling.

When he threw a third score, this time to Deion Branch, also off play-action, midway through the third quarter to make it 24-7, it left Philadelphia quarterback Donovan McNabb in the same position Brady was in a week ago. He was playing behind the 8-ball, a position that most often leads to mistakes and more misery. Not to mention some sleepless nights.

"I think we had great field position [because of the forced turnovers]," Brady said. "Our defense created great field position. We scored some points early off those turnovers to take the lead. At the point we went up 17 points, they're running uphill. With your back against the wall you can't use the full gamut of your playbook."

Jets
Injuries mount, but not excuses

23-16

NYJ	3	3	3	7
NE	3	3	10	7

FOXBOROUGH

The effects of mounting injuries may take their toll down the road, but for the second straight week, the New England Patriots looked the casts, wraps, and braces square in the eye and laughed. Rosevelt Colvin (hip) out for the season? Ted Johnson (foot) out until Week 12? Mike Compton out with a foot injury? Injuries during the game to Ted Washington (fractured left leg), David Patten (right leg), Mike

Then Brady and Co. arrived in Philadelphia and all was suddenly right with the world again. At least for the moment.

"I didn't sleep much this week," Brady said. "As a quarterback a lot of times you take pride in winning football games. When the team doesn't win and you get defeated, 31-0, and you throw four interceptions, and you get shut out for the first time in how many years, that's tough. At the same

time, you need confidence to believe in yourself."

Brady got some of that confidence back in a hurry when he capitalized on two Eagles turnovers in the second quarter and turned them into back-to-back touchdown passes off play-action fakes. Both times those fakes froze the defense for just long enough to allow tight end Christian Fauria to break free in the end zone. Both times Brady found him, as he had so often last

BREAKS A STREAK OF FIVE CONSECUTIVE DEFEATS BY THE PATRIOTS, DATING BACK TO WEEK 10 OF THE 2000 SEASON

Vrabel (arm injury, extent unknown), and Ty Law (right ankle sprain)?

It didn't matter.

The JVs stepped in and played just fine as the Patriots improved to 2-1 with a 23-16 win in their Gillette Stadium home opener, a game in which the Patriots turned Jets mistakes into points while the Jets failed to convert on New England's miscues.

It was nickel back Asante Samuel's 55-yard interception return for a touchdown to open the fourth quarter that ultimately did in the Jets (0-3). Vinny Testaverde, 39, made a terrible mistake and underthrew Wayne Chrebet, who slipped on his break, allowing Samuel to make the biggest play of his short NFL career, juggling the ball for a moment before running to paydirt.

"Coach made a good call and put me in the right position to make the play," said the rookie corner from Central Florida. "It was a good feeling. It made me feel like I was on Cloud Nine. I was man-to-man on Chrebet and he was shifting and shaking and I waited for him to make his break. I'd never returned one for a touchdown before. Every time I'd get to the 40 and the 30 and the 20, I'd say to myself, 'You're getting closer, keep going.'"

Oh, he kept going all right, leaving Testaverde, Chrebet, and Jets coach Herm Edwards with a sinking feeling. And yet, the Jets came back and pulled within a touchdown when a breakdown occurred in the New England secondary and Testaverde marched the Jets right down the Patriots' throats, culminating in a 29-yard strike to Chrebet with 12:53 left.

But that emptied the Jets' tank.

It was 9-9 (three field goals each by Adam Vinatieri and Doug Brien) when the Patriots marched it 73 yards in seven plays, highlighted by a wide open 28-yard gain on a Tom Brady-to-

Christian Fauria connection. On a second-and-10 from the 20, Brady threw toward Troy Brown in the end zone, and he drew an interference call on Ray Mickens, who was subbing for the injured Donnie Abraham. Mickens seemed to have great position, but he failed to turn to the ball. The ball was spotted at the 1, from where Brady, unable to find anyone open, skirted a pass rush and ran it in.

"I looked at my first read and he got caught up," Brady said. "The second guy was on the corner; he got caught up. And I looked back to Christian and he had a double team, so I kind of pumped and then fell into the end zone, it looked like. It wasn't a graceful run." ⟋

Redskins

Bitter pill as comeback fizzles

17 - 20

NE	3	0	7	7
WAS	3	3	14	0

LANDOVER, MD. Physically, there aren't many things you would say Tom Brady does better than the other 31 starting quarterbacks in the NFL. Many of them have stronger arms. Some are more accurate passers. All but a few are more nimble. And there may be a couple — Brett Favre and Steve McNair come to mind — who are as effective a leader.

But none is a more intense competitor. In fact, there may not be a player at any position who takes losing harder than the Patriots' young QB (though if he isn't careful, he'll grow old sooner

than he'd like).

That's why Brady needed a few extra moments to collect himself before leaving his locker for the interview room, where he would attempt to explain his throwing three interceptions and, for the first time in memory, failing to deliver in the clutch, leaving New England on the losing end of a

Deion Branch kept his hand in the victory over the Jets with a pair of catches.

20-17 game against the Washington Redskins.

Know this much: Those folding chairs in the visiting locker room at FedEx Field are pretty sturdy; they had to be to have supported Brady plus the weight of the world he seemed to be carrying on his slender shoulders long enough for him to memorize the

inside of his temporary quarters.

For the first two weeks of the season we've seen Brady shrug off persistent pain in his throwing elbow, but, judging by the look on his face and the way his voice quavered, it took every ounce of his pride to keep from shedding tears following a narrow defeat in which the Patriots faced fourth and 3

from Washington's 38 with 43 seconds to go. "Everyone's real disappointed," the Patriots' quarterback said. "More disappointment than we've had in a while because this is a game we really feel we should have won."

The Patriots trailed, 20-3, in the third quarter before rallying. They got within 20-17 when Brady directed a

68-yard drive that ended with a 7-yard scoring pass to Larry Centers with 2 minutes 10 seconds left. The Redskins imploded (three false starts) on their next possession, and New England got the ball back at Washington's 45 with 1:39 to go, needing only a first down to get into field-goal range.

Brady threw incomplete to Deion Branch on first down, to Centers for 5 yards on second down, and, following Centers's 2-yard run, he threw behind Daniel Graham deep down the middle.

Centers implied after the game that he was open near the first-down marker on New England's final play. "If you complete it, no foul, I'm not disappointed," Center said. "Sometimes you gotta know when to take that shot. I think Tom did a pretty good job for us, we just had some unfortunate things that didn't work out for us." ✐

Titans

Passing physical with flying colors

38-30

TEN	6	7	3	14
NE	7	0	14	17

FOXBOROUGH
While the Red Sox were "cowboying up" at Fenway Park, the Patriots were "knuckling up" at Gillette Stadium. That was their unofficial rallying cry. That is to say New England wasn't going to back down against one of the league's hardest-hitting teams. The Patriots came looking for a fight with the intention of taking it to Tennessee the way the Titans took it to them in December of 2002.

Ty Law ignored his severely sprained ankle to score the clinching touchdown on an interception.

Truth is, the Patriots took personally all the chatter about how physical Tennessee is. They didn't enjoy having folks come into their 'hood and remind them of how badly they'd been beaten (24-7) in Nashville. It's no wonder, then, the Patriots couldn't wait to catch the Titans on the block.

"They beat the [expletive] out of us last year," guard Damien Woody said. "The only way to put that away was to go out and return the favor."

The Patriots' 38-30 win was not pretty. Entertaining, perhaps, but not pretty. New England's offensive linemen were supposed to get overpowered. Instead, boosted by Woody's return, they handled Tennessee's talented defensive front to the tune of 161 rushing yards. Meanwhile, the Patriots' wounded defense shut down Eddie George and chased Steve McNair as if he had stolen something. And safety Rodney Harrison knocked guys around as though he had been involved in last year's loss.

Don't get it twisted. The Titans didn't just sit there and take it. The game featured seven lead changes. But in the end, after a fast and furious fourth quarter in which the teams combined to score 31 points, the Patriots were the last ones standing, improving to 3-2.

"All week, that's all we heard was how physical they were," said Harrison, who made a team-high 11 tackles, including a third-quarter hit that left Titans tight end Shad Meier with a concussion. "It was up to us to go out there and match their intensity. Going out there, one-on-one, and just knuckling up with those guys. They have a good team, a very tough team, but our guys played with a lot of heart and a lot of passion."

Perhaps no Patriot displayed more heart than Ty Law. Playing for the second week in a row with a severely sprained right ankle, Law was on the sideline for much of the second half, but talked his way back in time to snatch McNair's pass intended for Tyrone Calico and limp 65 yards with it for a touchdown that put New England ahead, 38-27, with 1 minute 49 seconds to go.

"I looked at [Law] and I told him, 'I know why you're the best,'" Harrison said. "To hurt his ankle and make a play like that to seal the victory, that was huge. And that just shows what type of player Ty Law is."

Giants

A victory only a coach could love

17 - 6

NYG	3	0	0	3
NE	7	0	10	0

FOXBOROUGH
This was more like it. Those shootouts, like the one they survived with Tennessee are OK once in a while, but that isn't Patriots football. Too, you know... pretty.

Their brand of ball is gritty. Grimy. Not attractive. Just effective. When they aren't a pleasure to watch, as the Giants learned on a muddy, rainy afternoon at Gillette Stadium, the Patriots can be a pain to play. New England won, 17-6. Had the score been 170-6, it still would have been anatomically impossible for Bill Belichick to wear a wider grin.

"Man, that was a great win for our football team," the Patriots coach said.

The Patriots didn't play great football. Offensively they didn't even play good football. But they played Patriots football. And that was good enough.

The defense forced five turnovers, including four Kerry Collins interceptions (two by Rodney Harrison) and a Tiki Barber fumble (forced by Tyrone Poole) that Matt Chatham returned 38 yards for a touchdown on the Giants' third play from scrimmage. The Giants had the ball for more than 10 more minutes, but the Patriots turned them away twice inside the 20-yard line and five other times inside New England's 30.

The Patriots converted just one of 11 third downs. But that one was a big one—a 21-yard completion from Tom Brady to David Givens on third-and-16 from the Patriots' 9 that kept alive their only touchdown drive. They had another solid game on the ground, gaining 129 yards on 31 attempts (4.2-yard average).

So no, it won't go down as one of the season's more memorable games, but this one fits in the only place that will matter come winter: the win column. "It was just a grind-it-out type game," guard Damien Woody said. "We're not the type of team that puts up 30 or 40 points every week. We're the type of team that grinds it out. We play good, solid defense and complementary offense. A lot of our wins are going to look like this."

"Right now we're just willing ourselves," Poole said.

The Patriots were killing themselves in the first half. They went three and out on five straight possessions and moved the ball 29 yards in 21 plays. Brady went 1 for 10. They managed one first down and committed six penalties. "That was not what we were looking for," Brady said.

Still they led, 7-3, at the break thanks to three New York turnovers and two missed field goals by Brett Conway. They would have had more

2001
Wide receiver Troy Brown had a team-record 101
receptions during the season.

2003
No Patriot receiver had double-digit
receptions in a single game.

Deion Branch's 11 catches in Super Bowl XXXIX

2004
Of David Givens' 56 receptions,
47 resulted in first downs.

tied the record held by the 49ers' Jerry Rice and the Bengals' Dan Ross.

Eugene Wilson, Chris Akins, and Anthony Pleasant make things anything but pleasant for the Dolphins' Ricky Williams

had they capitalized on Poole's interception of a Collins pass that was deflected by Richard Seymour on the first play from scrimmage. Adam Vinatieri missed a 42-yard field goal. (His fourth miss in his last six attempts. Worried yet?) "The defense was fantastic," Troy Brown said. "They kept us around until we had a chance to get something going." *

Dolphins

Over time, game went their way

19-13

NE	3	3	7	0	6
MIA	10	3	0	0	0

MIAMI
Sooner or later, the hex, the curse, or whatever it was had to end.

The streak had to end. And, unfortunately, a quality football game had to end. What a way to end them all.

Tom Brady threw an 82-yard touchdown pass to Troy Brown 9 minutes and 15 seconds into overtime at Pro Player Stadium to give the Patriots a thrilling 19-13 win — New England's first in 14 visits to Miami in September or October — only after Richard Seymour blocked Olindo Mare's attempt at a go-ahead field goal with two minutes remaining in regulation, Mare (the second-most-accurate kicker in league history) missed a 35-yarder in overtime wide right, Brady recovered his own fumble at New England's 40, and Tyrone Poole intercepted Jay Fiedler on Miami's second possession of the extra session.

"It was almost like they were trying

to give it to us," Brown said. "It was a matter of time before we took advantage of it."

Guess it was just time. Thirty-seven years was enough. Sixty-nine minutes was enough. The Patriots definitely had had enough of being punked in Miami.

"It was good to get that monkey off our back, coming down here to Miami and losing for I don't know how many years in a row [five]," Brown said after his walk-off touchdown vaulted New England into first place in the AFC East by a half-game over the Dolphins. "It feels good just to come down here and get a win. It was one of those things hanging over our heads. We've been in a couple of those situations. The Jet thing, coming to New England and beating us up for four or five years [five, actually]. Coming down here and losing for I don't know how many years in a row in September. Another one of those things to get off your back. Hopefully, next year you guys won't hang it over our heads."

Can't. They've got another streak going. The Patriots have beaten the Dolphins in overtime the last two times they've met. New England overcame a 24-13 deficit with five minutes left in last season's finale to win, 27-24, and keep the Dolphins out of the playoffs. As they did last December, the Dolphins had several opportunities to put the Patriots away. They didn't. Or, worse for their annually failed Super Bowl aspirations, they couldn't.

Miami's Jason Taylor beat Matt Light inside, but Damien Woody was there to back Light up. Brady, having play-faked and pump-faked right, drifted left and—sore elbow, sore shoulder, and all—heaved a deep pass to Brown, whose post route across the field split Dolphin safeties Sammy Knight and Brock Marion. Miami was in a two-deep zone. The Dolphins let

Brown get too deep and he ended up scoring.

"Brady, I don't know how long he held onto the ball," Dolphins coach Dave Wannstedt said, "but he throws it on time, [Brown's] not going to get behind [the coverage]." *

Browns

A break from the schedule-maker

9-3

CLE	0	3	0	0
NE	3	0	3	3

FOXBOROUGH
Halfway through the regular season the time had come for the bruised and battered Patriots to finally catch a break.

They got it in the form of a Cleveland team whose preferred quarterback, Kelly Holcomb, has a broken right fibula — a bleeding broken right fibula, actually — so painful he could not start, though he was pressed into action when starter Tim Couch sprained his right thumb near the end of the first half. A team without its stud running back, former Boston College star William Green, who sat with an injured right shoulder. A team without three of its opening-day starters on the offensive line.

"Join the club, buddy," Tedy Bruschi said. "It's not a matter of who's down but who's in there and are they getting the job done."

That, in a nutshell, is the story of New England's season, one that at the midpoint has them 6-2 for the fifth time in franchise history and leading

Kevin Faulk busted through with a career-high 96 yards rushing vs. Cleveland.

the AFC East. Getting the job done was Kevin Faulk, who contributed 154 yards from scrimmage, a career-high 96 rushing. Putting in work was second-year tight end Daniel Graham with seven catches for 110 yards, easily the best game of his career. Owed time and a half is a New England defense that allowed Cleveland to reach midfield twice and has allowed one TD in its last three games. Earning his check was Mike Vrabel with a career-high three sacks and a forced fumble vs. the team he grew up supporting. Employee of the day: Special teams coach Brad Seely, whose unit accounted for all the Patriots' points and downed four Ken Walter punts inside the 20.

There are some concerns in this week's evaluation, namely the offense's struggles in the red zone (0 for 3) and

on third down (4 for 14). But the crew won its fourth in a row and sixth in seven. Boss Belichick is pleased.

"That was really about the way we expected that game to go," Bill Belichick said of his second win in three tries against his former team, this one not a done deal until Ty Law intercepted Holcomb with less than a minute to go. "Cleveland is a team that has been in a lot of close games. That's usually what it comes down to and that's certainly what it came down to today — last possession of the game."

"Some of these weeks we're going to need to score a lot more points than we did," acknowledged Tom Brady, who got the offense to the doorstep of the red zone (the 20) late in the fourth quarter before looking to Vinatieri to salvage 3 from 38. "We had some op-

portunities, but we really just didn't take advantage. At some point, that's going to bite you in the butt." ⬭

Broncos
Strategic safety sets the stage

30 - 26

NE	7	6	7	10
DEN	7	10	7	2

DENVER

Patriots coach Bill Belichick always talks about how turnovers and penalties decide games. And he's right. Turnovers and penalties do decide games.

Most games. Not this game.

Despite turning the ball over twice and committing a season-high 14 penalties at Invesco Field at Mile High, the Patriots overcame the Denver Broncos, 30-26, on Tom Brady's 18-yard touchdown pass to David Givens with 30 seconds remaining in front of 72,852 mostly stunned witnesses.

The win was the fifth in a row for New England (7-2) and, coupled with Miami's loss to Indianapolis Sunday, widened its AFC East lead to 1½ games. The win was only the Patriots' second in their last 14 trips to the Mile High City, but they've won two of three games here under Belichick.

It's not often that the key play in a victory involves the other team scoring and expanding its lead. But that's what happened in this one. With 2:51 remaining and the Broncos leading, 24-23, the Patriots lined up to punt from their 1. But rather than have Ken Walter kick and give Denver prime field position, Belichick and special teams coach Brad Seely had long snapper Lonie Paxton — a potential goat just a quarter earlier — snap the ball out of the end zone.

The intentional safety made it 26-23, Denver, and set up a Patriots free kick from the 30. Deltha O'Neal misplayed Walter's kick, and Denver took over on its own 15. "That's 25, 30 yards of field position," Broncos coach Mike Shanahan said.

"We just made one more play than they did," Belichick said. "We've got a lot of tough guys in that locker room. It was tough out there, but those guys are tough, too. This team is a pretty resilient team. We just wanted to come out of here with a victory."

After forcing the Broncos to go three and out, the Patriots took possession at their 42 with 2:15 left and one timeout. They wouldn't need it.

In six plays and 1:30, Brady drove his team 58 yards, 42 coming on completions to Faulk. On first down from the Denver 18, Brady intentionally threw to the front corner of the end-zone behind Givens, who made the adjustment and the catch just inside the left pylon. The irony was that Givens was being defended by O'Neal, who had given Denver a 24-20 lead with a 57-yard punt return.

Brady, who had struggled in his first two games against Denver, completed 20 of 35 passes for 350 yards and three touchdowns. ⊘

Deion Branch caught three passes for 107 yards against Denver, getting behind the defense for this 66-yard touchdown reception.

Cowboys

In Battle of Bills, better team wins

12-0

DAL	0	0	0	0
NE	3	6	0	3

FOXBOROUGH

Before the game, no matter how hard Bill Belichick and Bill Parcells fought to escape the spotlight, it really was all about them. Do the two of you speak? Will you speak? How do you feel about Bill? And how do you feel about Bill? What did you learn from Bill? Are you still angry at Bill?

After the game, it was still all about them. Look, they hugged each other. What did he say? What did he say? What does this win mean to you, Bill? What does this loss mean to you, Bill?

In between, though, it really was all about the players. Just like the coaches said. And right now, Belichick has a better collection of them.

His Patriots improved to 8-2 for the second time in franchise history (1978) and maintained their two-game lead in the AFC East with a 12-0 victory over the Cowboys before a national television audience and 68,436 at Gillette Stadium. The shutout was New England's first since the third game of the 1996 season, when Parcells coached the Patriots and Belichick was his assistant, and the second time Dallas has been held scoreless in its last four games.

Dallas amassed more total yards and held a slight edge in time of pos-session, but turned the ball over three times, once inside the Patriots 20.

Tom Brady completed just 15 of 34 passes, but completions of 57 yards to David Givens and 46 yards to Deion Branch led to 9 points. His counterpart, Quincy Carter, threw three intercep-tions, including one in the third quarter to Ty Law with Dallas 19 yards away from making it a 2-point game.

And yes, they did embrace.

"Bill congratulated me on the win," Belichick said. "I told him I thought he had a good football team and I wished him well, and I do."

And as far as the Patriots' coach was concerned, thus ended the Battle of the Bills.

After the game, an embrace and best wishes were exchanged by the former coaching compatriots.

"Coach Belichick told us to enjoy this win," said Law, who finished with a pair of interceptions, "but he reminded us that Houston is a tough team. They went up there to Buffalo and did something we didn't do, and that's beat those guys [12-10]."

"All the players knew this was big for him," guard Damien Woody said. "We're happy for him. It's one more step in the right direction for the organization."

"It's good to beat the teacher," said defensive coordinator Romeo Crennel, also a former Parcells employee. "We feel good about that. But our main focus is that we have to go to Houston next week."

The Cowboys offense had its share of problems. Dallas managed a mere 3 yards per carry and Carter struggled to a 38.0 quarterback rating. New England's defense did a lot less bending than usual.

"They played a lot better than we did," Parcells said. "We just didn't give ourselves a chance to win the game. I thought maybe there in the third quarter, where we had that one decent drive in there, if we could have got on the board there, we might have made it close. As it happened all night, we just kind of self-destructed."

"We just tried to play physical, tried to get up in [Terry Glenn's] face and attack him at the line of scrimmage," Law said, applying New England's general game plan specifically to his former teammate and friend.

"You don't want to let him find soft spots in the zone," Law continued. "Because once he gets running, it's probably going to be hard to catch him. Granted, he's probably faster than the majority of us out there; we have to stop him any way we can. The only way you can beat speed is with strength, and that's the way you hold the guy down."

Texans

Unlikely scramble, improbable win

23 - 20

NE	0	10	0	10	3
HOU	3	0	7	10	0

HOUSTON

A tough few days for Tom Brady: His apartment was burglarized and he lost a television. Two of his passes were stolen by the Texans and he lost a fumble. He also got pancaked near his own end zone in overtime.

But he's Tom Brady and somewhere along the line the football gods sprinkled stardust on his shoulder pads. There's always another TV to be delivered and there's always another victory to be won after the game appears lost. When you are Tom Brady the road of landmines always leads to somewhere over the rainbow.

In yet another seemingly hopeless late-game situation, Brady overcame some uncharacteristic mistakes and led the Patriots to a 23-20 overtime victory over the Houston Texans before 70,719 10-gallon-mad-hatters at Reliant Stadium.

Brady's gaudy numbers included 29 completions in 47 attempts for a whopping 368 yards and two touchdowns, but those don't really tell you much about what kind of a day this was for QB 12.

This was a game in which Brady made some old-fashioned Bledsoe-like blunders—trying to do too much when he'd have been better off eating the football. It was a game in which the Patriots annihilated the Texans in every offensive category except points.

Brady gets much of the blame for the shortcomings, but he scrambled when he had to scramble, and converted third-down and fourth-down plays in the fourth quarter and OT when he had to make them, and somehow he willed his team to victory. Again. With Brady at quarterback, the Patriots are 7-0 in overtime games.

Adam Vinatieri gave the Texans the boot, kicking the winning field goal with 41 seconds left in overtime.

"It didn't look good there for a while," the Pats' QB said. "But it showed you we've got a lot of heart and perseverance."

After a day of mistakes and failures to capitalize, the Patriots trailed, 20-13, and faced a third-and-10 from their 33 with 2:26 left when Brady dropped back to pass and saw nothing.

His receivers were all covered and there were linemen in his face. At that moment, he did something very un-Brady like. He scrambled.

Brady is not Doug Flutie. Brady scrambling looks as natural as Bob Kraft dancing with Ty Law at City Hall Plaza. But he eluded his pursuers and gave Daniel Graham time to get open. He finally got it to Graham downfield for a game-saving 33-yard completion.

"I was running for my life," Brady explained. "The first couple of guys weren't open. I had to spin back and roll to my right. I saw Daniel lose his guy and I just threw it. I didn't see the completion."

The big gain set up (five plays later) a fourth-and-14-yard touchdown pass to Graham with 40 seconds left that sent the game into OT.

The TD required more improvisation from New England's signal-caller. He ran a bootleg to his right, but the Texans hadn't gone for the fake run to the left and it was clear Brady was going to lose his footrace for the first down. Instead of letting the game end on the play, he threw off his back foot, against the flow, and lofted it over coverage and into the suddenly dependable hands of Graham.

In overtime, Brady could have lost the game again, but somehow he held on to the ball when he was blindsided by Jamie Sharper on a third-and-6 from his 13.

A fumble would have meant the end of New England's six-game winning streak, but Brady held on, the Patriots punted, and they lived for another possession.

On the winning drive, Brady took the Patriots from their 14 down to the Houston 10, setting up Adam Vinatieri's field goal with just 41 seconds left in OT. The win gave Brady a career regular-season record (as a starter) of 29-12, which leads all active quarterbacks. ⌀

When the dust cleared on the goal-line stand, the Patriots and Eugene Wilson (26) were riding high.

Colts

Defense shines in 'The Longest Yard'

38-34

NE	10	14	7	7
IND	0	10	14	10

INDIANAPOLIS

Down the Atlantic coast in Charlotte, N.C., they like to call their Carolina Panthers the "Cardiac Cats." Yeah. The Panthers have been known to pull out a close win here and there this year. But, man oh man. They've got nothing on New England's "Palpitation Pats."

For goodness' sake, the Patriots nearly lost their starting left guard in the final fast-and-furious moments of a 38-34 victory in Week 12 at the RCA Dome in which they denied the Colts the winning touchdown three times from the 1-yard line. "I was about to have a heart attack out there," Damien Woody said. He didn't, obviously, although Colts fans are suffering from a severe case of heartache after their team's rally from a 21-point second-half deficit fell short.

As for the Patriots, another week, another way to win. There's getting to be lots of variety in the "New Releases" section of the video room back at Gillette Stadium. You've got your action/adventure flicks, such as "Tennessee" and "Miami." Your love story in "Dallas." And your mystery/suspense thrillers like "Denver," "Houston," and now "Indianapolis."

The Colts had an alternate ending planned when they got the ball at New England's 48 with 2:57 to go. But Willie McGinest and Ted Washington ruined the scene by stuffing Edgerrin

James on fourth and goal from the 1 with 14 seconds to go.

With that, New England avoided its first loss since Sept. 28. The "Palpitation Pats" have won eight straight and lead the AFC East by two games heading into next week's division championship game against the Dolphins at Gillette Stadium. A victory and New England (10-2) clinches its second division title in three seasons.

This game was the Patriots' fourth in six weeks to be decided in the final minute of regulation or overtime. We all knew the defense could bend without breaking. Just not that far. "I'm sitting here, still exhausted and totally surprised at what happened," Rodney Harrison said. "The way this team continues to dig deep inside and find ways to win. Unbelievable. I've never been a part of something like this."

As it turned out, this game was decided three weeks ago, during the bye week, when the Patriots paid extra attention to their goal-line defense. "We couldn't stop anybody the first half of the season," coach Bill Belichick said.

The Patriots couldn't stop the Colts in the second half of this game, until they absolutely had to. Following a curious selection of play calls (Indianapolis was down to its final timeout with about 3½ minutes left, yet the Patriots passed three times — all incompletions) and an 18-yard punt by Ken Walter, the Colts took over at New England's 48 with 2:57 left. Six plays later, it was first and goal at the 2.

Tedy Bruschi and Mike Vrabel combined to hold James to a 1-yard gain on first down. Clock running. The Colts hurried to run the next play, but Bruschi was there again, this time with help from Harrison, to stuff James for no gain.

On or near the goal line is when teams usually run their goal-line offenses. But promising rookie full-back/tight end Dallas Clark, fullback Detron Smith, and occasional fullback James Mungro all were hurt, so the Colts had little choice but to remain in their three-receiver package. "We didn't have 'goal line' because the whole team is hurt," Colts quarterback Peyton Manning said. "We had no fullback and no tight end. That's what it came down to.

We had no personnel options."

For third down they brought in 6-foot-3-inch rookie receiver Aaron Moorehead. Tyrone Poole, the Patriots' 5-8 corner and a former Colt, guessed fade. He guessed right. Incomplete.

Fourth down. Fourteen seconds to go. Three feet to go. The Colts were still in their three-receiver set. McGinest was back in the game after leaving a play earlier with what he said was a left knee injury, although Belichick said McGinest was "cramping up."

McGinest had left the field to boos from most of the 57,102 at the RCA Dome for delaying the game. He would leave again to cheers from the Patriots fans in the crowd for making the play that decided the game. ✍

Dolphins

One goal realized, but much left to do

12-0

MIA	0	0	0	0
NE	3	0	0	9

FOXBOROUGH
Success won't change the Patriots. Better yet, success in December won't change the Patriots.

"We've got big plans," said rookie safety Eugene Wilson. "[This is] the first step."

New England secured its second AFC East title in three seasons with a 12-0 win over the Miami Dolphins at a giant snow globe commonly known as Gillette Stadium.

If the players celebrated over any of this, they kept it brief and conducted it before outsiders were allowed into their locker room. They left the fun to the 45,378 fans, who following Tedy Bruschi's fourth-quarter touchdown used the snow that caused major logistical problems for party favors, tossing it skyward in unison. Honestly, the only visible proof that the players had accomplished anything was their commemorative T-shirts.

Blame it on Bill Belichick. The coach's tunnel-vision approach has seen the Patriots through 11 victories in 12 games and nine consecutive wins, so who are we to suggest an alternative?

In the postgame locker room, he congratulated his team, told it to savor its first season sweep of Miami since 1997.

"Everything trickles down from Coach Belichick," said Antowain Smith, who went from the inactive list to carrying 27 times. "He's not going to let us get too high. The main thing he told us was to be humble, that it's a great victory for us, and not to take anything away from ourselves. But the job is not complete yet."

"He keeps putting goals up there for you," offensive lineman Damien Woody said. "You never want to stay the same. You want to keep going up. He always puts goals in front of us. Even after a victory like this, the goal now is to maintain the No. 1 seed and beat a Jacksonville squad that's on the rise."

Belichick did not entertain any discussion before the game about the possibility that his team would clinch

Tedy Bruschi scored the game's lone touchdown on a fourth-quarter interception return.

a division title sooner than any other in franchise history.

After it was done, he had little to say about it.

"It's one of your goals at the beginning of the year," said Belichick, whose team has won 11 games, which ties it for the most regular-season wins in Patriots history. "We're happy about it, obviously, but there's still a lot of football left to be played this year. We'll just keep looking ahead. I saw Jacksonville had a really big win and I watched a little bit of them on tape this week. They're pretty good, especially defensively. This will be a good challenge for us. We have to put this one behind us and move ahead. We'll enjoy it for a couple of hours."

It was not an enjoyable three hours for Miami, the fifth opponent New England has held to 10 points or fewer this season and the second straight visitor to Gillette Stadium not to score. (Tennessee's Steve McNair, four home games and two months ago, was the last person to score a touchdown here.) If you don't think this season is special, consider that the Patriots, coming into the season, had not shut out an opponent since 1996.

Jaguars

Homing in on playoff placement

27-13

JACK	3	3	0	7
NE	7	6	0	14

FOXBOROUGH

Now it's all up to the Jets and Bills to rescue the other AFC contenders' Super Bowl chances. The Chiefs, Colts, Titans, Broncos, Bengals, Ravens, and Dolphins all are depending on you, New York and Buffalo, to do something in the next two weeks to keep New England from claiming home-field advantage in the playoffs. Because lately, only the Patriots have been able to do much of anything at Gillette Stadium.

Their 27-13 taming of the Jacksonville Jaguars in Week 14 was a franchise-record 10th in succession and 12th of the regular season, also a team record. The Patriots have not lost since Sept. 28 at Washington and, worse if you're a prospective playoff opponent, they haven't lost at home since the Jets beat them in December 2002, a run of 10 games, including exhibitions. The win improved the Patriots' home record to 7-0 this season.

For those teams who have a realistic chance to be in Houston Feb. 1, Foxborough is not the place they want to be in January.

At least one team will have no choice should the Patriots beat the Jets at the Meadowlands Saturday night; a win would clinch a first-round bye and a divisional playoff game at home. If the 12-2 Patriots win their last two games, they'll be the AFC's top seed in

David Givens helps the Patriots extend their team-record winning streak to 10.

the postseason.

Bill Belichick likes to remind us that no one can control the weather, but his team has little difficulty controlling games at Gillette when the weather is not conducive to picnics in the park. The Patriots are 6-0 all-time when snow falls (2-0 in the last two weeks) in Foxborough and 13-2 in the last 10 years when the temperature dips to 35 degrees or below. (It was 25 degrees at game time and the snow started in the third quarter.) To the best of our knowledge, it's not expected to get warmer in these parts in the coming weeks. If you find that it does, pray for cold.

Come to think of it, divine intervention may be opponents' best weapon when they must venture into the "White Hole."

"That's the environment we want it to be," guard Damien Woody said of what may be the league's biggest home-field advantage. "Win these last two games and have home field throughout the playoffs here? People are going to catch hell coming up here to play. We're at home, we're in front of our own crowd. That's a great situation to be in. We know it's a tough place to play if you're an opponent."

According to Elias Sports Bureau, the Patriots were the first team not to allow a touchdown in four straight home games since the 1938 New York Giants. Had the streak reached five games, New England would have tied the 1932 Chicago Bears. Both the Giants in '38 and the Bears in '32 went on to win the NFL championship, by the way.

The Jets effectively won the AFC East championship in 2002 as guests of Gillette Stadium in the second-to-last game of the season. Belichick will remind his team of that, to be certain. Just missing a third consecutive home shutout meant about as much to him

THE GAME FOR THE FIRST TIME SINCE SEPTEMBER 2002; THEY'VE ALLOWED ONLY ONE TD IN LAST FIVE HOME GAMES

late yesterday afternoon as the Jaguars game that had just finished.

"Right now, we're going on the road against the Jets, a division game," Belichick said. "Our last two road division games, against Buffalo and Miami, were two of the toughest games of the year. That will be a big challenge for us and that's really what we're looking ahead toward. Those streaks or whatever they are, I'm not really too concerned about those." ◯

Jets
Toughest remaining hurdle is cleared

21-16

NE	7	7	7	0
NYJ	7	3	0	6

EAST RUTHERFORD Based on the history of this series, if there was a game that posed the biggest threat to the Patriots' winning streak, "Jets at the Meadowlands" was the one.

The threat was real, but the streak remains intact.

The 2003 Patriots extended their franchise record with their 11th straight, a 21-16 takedown of the Jets before a national television audience and 77,835 at the Meadowlands.

It was again the Patriots defense that made the difference. The Patriots intercepted Jets quarterback Chad Pennington five times, including one that Willie McGinest returned 15 yards for a touchdown in the second quarter that gave the Patriots a lead they would hold for the rest of the evening. Another of Pennington's picks,

by Tedy Bruschi, led to New England's first touchdown. Still another, Ty Law's pick in the end zone in the third quarter, ended a Jets scoring threat. Safeties Rodney Harrison and Eugene Wilson also had interceptions.

"Getting those scores early, that was important," coach Bill Belichick said. "We were able to play most of the game from ahead, which was good."

Bruschi's leaping interception over the middle on New York's second play from scrimmage gave the Patriots possession at the Jets' 35. On the next play, Tom Brady and David Givens collaborated on a 35-yard touchdown, giving the Patriots a 7-0 lead 48 seconds into the game.

New England did not score a touchdown on its first possession in its first 13 games. The Patriots have done it two weeks in a row.

Givens would later catch his team-leading fifth touchdown of the season, a 5-yarder on the first drive of the third quarter.

The Patriots' early lead didn't last long, however. Pennington responded by directing the Jets on a 16-play, 83-yard drive that ate up 9 minutes 20 seconds and ended with his 1-yard touchdown run. The Patriots had the play-action pass covered well on third and goal but Pennington kept rolling out until he reached the end zone.

McGinest broke the 7-7 tie with his interception return 1:26 into the second quarter. On third and 2 from his 15, Pennington tried to hit Curtis Conway on a slant. McGinest, in perfect position, used his 6-foot-5-inch frame to leap and deflect the pass. A la Asante Samuel in Game 3, McGinest caught the deflection and took it to the end zone. It was the Patriots' league-leading sixth defensive touchdown of the season.

With 1:55 to go before intermission, the Jets took over at their 25. Eighty-

four seconds later, they were at New England's 5, but the Jets had to settle for Doug Brien's 29-yard field goal and a 4-point deficit at halftime.

Pennington, who scored both New York touchdowns on runs of 1 and 10 yards, never had thrown more than two interceptions in any of his first 26 games (19 starts). The Jets' five turnovers equaled a third of their giveaways through their first 14 games — 15, the second-fewest in the league.

The previous time the Patriots faced Pennington, he picked them apart, passing for 285 yards and three touchdowns. That was last year, before Bill Belichick overhauled his secondary. In the rematch, Pennington just got picked. And picked. And picked.

"We tried to disguise a lot, move around a lot," Harrison said. "To be honest with you, you can disguise all you want against good quarterbacks, but it comes down to guys making plays." ◯

Bills
Turnabout is fair play

31-0

BUF	0	0	0	0
NE	14	14	0	3

FOXBOROUGH Home-field advantage throughout the playoffs. Revenge. Offensive and defensive domination. An 8-0 record at Gillette Stadium. A 14-2 regular-season record.

The closest thing to a perfect season, and the Patriots' best regular season ever, concluded at Gillette Stadium

with a poetic 31-0 splattering of the Buffalo Bills. Buffalo appeared to pack it in even before the opening whistle and never challenged the Patriots, who won their 12th straight game.

The score was sweet revenge, matching the Week 1 thrashing of the Patriots by the Bills.

The Patriots' third shutout of the season was preserved by a Larry Izzo interception of Bills backup quarterback Travis Brown in the end zone with 13 seconds remaining.

"All 53 guys wanted to keep that zero on the scoreboard," said Izzo. "You have to give credit to everyone in this locker room. It wasn't just one play. It was 60 minutes of football."

There was no Gatorade splash of coach Bill Belichick late in the game. There was no large celebration in the locker room. This is a team that knows that if it doesn't win the Super Bowl,

the regular season doesn't mean much.

The game showed the opposite paths former teammates Tom Brady and Drew Bledsoe are on. Bledsoe was 12 for 29 for 83 yards with one interception. Brady was 21 for 32 for 204 yards and threw four touchdowns in the first half. It was a rather sad performance by Bledsoe (34.7 rating in the game), one of the troika of personalities who saved Patriots football in the early '90s along with owner Robert Kraft and former Patriots coach Bill Parcells.

"Some people might look at the scoreboard and say Buffalo laid down. They fought hard and we whupped them," said linebacker Matt Chatham.

If that was the case on the field, it didn't look that way from afar. It looked like Bledsoe was on an island, and the New England defense was in a feeding frenzy. It held the Bills to 256 yards and the time of possession

was almost seven minutes in New England's favor.

Already trailing, 7-0, Bledsoe was hit as he threw his first pass of the game when Tedy Bruschi roared in on a blitz. Bledsoe's dying quail was picked off by Mike Vrabel and returned 14 yards to the Bills 34.

From there, the Patriots scored their second touchdown on a 9-yard pass from Brady to Bethel Johnson.

"It all happened pretty fast," said Johnson, a rookie who became one of Brady's favorite targets. "I don't know what coverage they were in, but they were pretty much leaving me out there by myself the whole time. Tom just recognized it and threw it on in."

The Patriots and tight end Daniel Graham were on a forward roll in the season finale.

SA

2001
The Patriots had five fewer sacks
than their opponents.

2003
The Patriots ranked 6th in
the NFL with 41 sacks, led by
Mike Vrabel with $9\frac{1}{2}$.

POSTSEASON The Pats had four sacks in Super Bowl XXXIX

2004
New England tied for third in the
league with 45 sacks, led by Willie
McGinest with $9\frac{1}{2}$.

vs. the Eagles, which ties for the second-most in team playoff history.

BY JACKIE MACMULLAN

BRUSCHI

A PERFECT FIT FOR THE PATRIOTS

He caught the ball precisely the way it was diagrammed.

Tedy Bruschi was elated. This was exactly what he'd worked toward, a big play in a big game to prove to his coach, Bill Parcells, that he belonged on this football team, that he wasn't too short, or too slight, or too young to be an impact player.

He knew Parcells had been hesitant to draft him. He was used to doubters surveying him at a shade over 6 feet, and 245 pounds, and wondering aloud how he would ever be able to rush the quarterback successfully. Bruschi wanted to play defensive end in college, but the recruiters kept politely correcting him. No, son. You won't be able to do that at the next level.

When the Arizona staff agreed to give the kid a shot at his desired position, he promised them they would never regret it. He immersed himself in the middle of a defensive crew called the "Desert Swarm," and tied the all-time Division 1A record for career quarterback sacks with 52.

The pro scouts told him again he was too small to be a defensive end, and this time, Bruschi was forced to listen. The New England Patriots drafted him in the third round, prepared to use him on special teams and specific third-down situations.

So there he was, in 1996, playing for the Patriots in a pivotal game against the Broncos, and Parcells was calling for a fake punt. Tom Tupa performed his role beautifully, winding up as if to boom the ball down the field, before jerking the ball away, and tossing it to Bruschi, the rookie.

It was absolutely perfect — until Bruschi dropped the ball.

"That was the low point of my career," Bruschi said. "I had it. I had it in the bread basket, and someone knocked it out."

Defensive coordinator Al Groh groaned. He stood 8 feet away from his pupil on the sideline, tapping him on the helmet as he came off the field.

"You could see how badly it hurt him," Groh said. "It was so unusual he dropped it, because usually when you gave Tedy a job, he did it right. He took pride in that."

As he retreated to the sideline Bruschi looked up to see Parcells towering over him.

"Hold onto the ball!" Parcells growled. "Hold onto the damn ball!"

EARNING A REPUTATION

Bruschi has been in the league eight years now. He has eight career interceptions, and became the first linebacker in team history to return two interceptions for touchdowns last season. He did it again this year, including the aerial snag he made against Miami Dec. 7 that unleashed an impromptu snow shower among the euphoric Patriots fans.

Bruschi also finished second in tackles (127) behind Rodney Harrison. He is not a situational player.

"He's a perpetual motion machine," teammate Ted Johnson said. "His energy is undeniable. It's always there. And he has this inner confidence."

"I'm no longer an NFL guy," said Groh, who coaches the University of Virginia, "but I've got to believe he's one of the best players in the league."

"He is someone," said defensive end Richard Seymour, "who knows how to make big plays."

He is someone who has learned how to hold onto the ball.

"I can't tell you how many times I've gone back to that play against Denver," said Bruschi. "Whenever I start feeling really good about myself, I remember that game. I remember where I came from. And I get to work again."

Bruschi is no longer underrated, underappreciated, or undervalued. He has come to symbolize the spirit and heart of this 2003 Patriots team as it prepares a run for the Super Bowl, beginning against Tennessee.

Unlike 2001, when New England stunned the heavily favored St. Louis Rams to win its first championship, the Patriots are the trendy team now. They are now expected to win, and players like Tedy Bruschi are expected to perform.

This is not a problem. Bruschi tackles each game, Johnson says, "with a certain joie de vivre. He loves to play."

Almost nine years ago, Groh went to the East-West college All-Star game to watch his son Michael. He left with images of Bruschi pulsating in his head.

"I was immediately intrigued by him," Groh said. "I noticed two things. The first was how everyone from the West team gravitated toward Tedy. They had only been together four or five days, but here was this bunch of All-Stars, looking to this guy as their leader. The second thing was his un-bridled enthusiasm for the game. It was hard to miss. He performed in their practice like he was in the middle of a playoff game, and that was eye-catching."

Groh reported his findings to Parcells. Assistant coach Bill Belichick watched film of Bruschi and liked what he saw. Parcells deferred to his two respected colleagues, but still had questions about Bruschi's lack of size.

"I couldn't blame Bill," Groh said. "You looked at him, and you said, 'OK, he's this height, he's this weight, where on earth would this guy work?' I wasn't sure where, but my feeling was, 'Let's not dismiss him.'"

As soon as the Patriots drafted him, Bruschi identified the two daunting tasks in front of him: a new position to learn, and a new coach to convince.

"I remember the call well," said Bruschi, smiling. "The person on the phone said, 'Tedy, here is Bill Parcells.' Bill got on and said, 'Tedy, we're going to try you at linebacker. Here's Al Groh.' And that was it."

NATURAL INSTINCTS

His first days in camp were a jumble of confusion. When the coaches told him to pick up the hook (a receiver curling into the middle of the field), Bruschi looked at them blankly. Yet he compensated for his inexperience with a plethora of other traits that Belichick quickly identified.

"He was very quick, very smart, very instinctive," Belichick said. "You can ask him to do something he's never done before, and then you watch him, and you find yourself saying, 'For a guy that's never done it, that's not bad.' So you give him something else, and he does that, too."

"You have to give Al Groh and Bill Belichick all the credit for Tedy Bruschi," Parcells said. "They saw something, and developed a role for him."

His teammates have gravitated to-ward him much the way they did in that college All-Star game. Bruschi was an emotional spokesman when Lawyer Milloy was released.

He is the boss of a close-knit corps of linebackers. He is behind many practical jokes, including the one where a podium was strategically placed in front of linebacker Mike Vrabel's locker the day after he had a big game against Cleveland, and was summoned to the interview room.

"I knew it was Tedy," Vrabel said. "I didn't even have to ask."

As he's evolved into an elite defender — one who shifted first from defensive end to outside linebacker, then in 2002 to the inside — he has helped establish a new trend toward sleeker, smaller, quicker linebackers.

"Bill [Belichick] and I were talking about this the other day," said Parcells. "Tedy is sort of a hybrid player. Guys like him, who are versatile, dedicated, able to do different things, aren't that plentiful in this league. I've got [middle linebacker] Dat Nguyen in Dallas, but even he's a little different from Bruschi."

Nguyen is different because he played linebacker in college. Few, if any, of the other hybrid linebackers made the switch from defensive end.

"I guess that's what I sort of hang my hat on," Bruschi said. "Maybe I was one of the first so-called 'projects' that really opened the door for other guys. When the All-Pro team came out, you had [Baltimore linebacker] Ray Lewis, who is on a different level. But the other first-team guy was [Miami linebacker] Zach Thomas, and the second-team guys were me and Dat Nguyen. All three of us are a little undersized. I was like, 'Yeah, guys, we did it.'"

EARNING REDEMPTION

Hold onto the ball. He has come so far since then. Told that Bruschi still dwells on that play from his rookie year, Groh said the one he remembers from that season was in the AFC Championship against Jacksonville.

"It had snowed about 20 inches," Groh recalled. "Back then, [quarterback] Mark Brunell was still a pretty active quarterback. We were in a defensive scheme called 5 Robber. Because of Tedy's excellent athletic ability, and his instincts, he was the 'robber.'

"If Brunell ran, Tedy would hunt him down. But if Brunell stayed in the pocket, Tedy was to sit back as the 'robber' and try to steal anything he could in pass coverage.

"I remember the play very well. When Brunell dropped back, Tedy had his eyes fixed right on him. I just knew he was going to pick it off."

Bruschi intercepted Brunell's pass, ran it 12 yards up the field, then clutched the football close as his teammates mobbed him from the sideline. Parcells, with a hint of a smile, nodded his approval.

"That play brought some closure for me," Bruschi said. "It was in the same area of the field as the ball I dropped, right in front of our bench. When I held onto the ball, I said to myself, 'OK. Poetic justice.'"

New England was spanked by Green Bay in the Super Bowl that season. Parcells left to coach the Jets and took Belichick and Groh with him.

Would Parcells have ever guessed after his one and only year with Bruschi that the kid would turn into a second-team All-Pro linebacker?

"No, I don't think I could have ever determined that," Parcells admitted. "Back then, you loved his attitude, and you hoped he could help you, but he's exceeded everything you could have ever expected. Because of what he's done, other teams look at the Patriots and say, 'Maybe we could use a guy like Bruschi on our team.' That's the highest compliment I could give him." ⌀

The hold, the follow-through and the kick are picture-perfect as Adam Vinatieri sinks the Titans.

All they expected

"Everybody is 0-0 now," Bill Belichick said as soon as the regular season ended. "We all know what it is. Lose, and you are out. Win and you keep going."

Titans

Just as advertised, a Titanic struggle

TENN	7	0	7	0
NE	7	7	0	3

FOXBOROUGH
Give him credit. He called it.

Bill Belichick predicted that the AFC divisional playoff game at Gillette Stadium against the Tennessee Titans would be the Patriots' toughest game of the season. It sounded like a cliche when he said it. But Belichick couldn't have been more accurate.

Playing in the coldest game in franchise history (4 degrees, minus-10 windchill at kickoff), the top-seeded Patriots held on for a 17-14 win over the wild-card Titans. Adam Vinatieri, who had missed a 44-yard field goal in the first quarter, gave New England its 13th straight win with a 46-yarder with 4 minutes 6 seconds to play.

The Titans made it interesting on their last possession, driving 36 yards to New England's 40 before self-destructing after the two-minute warning. First, Tennessee was penalized 10 yards for intentional grounding by Steve McNair. Guard Benji Olson's holding penalty pushed the Titans back another 10 yards and put them in a third-and-22 situation.

McNair threw 10 yards to Drew Bennett on third down. On fourth and 12 from New England's 42, Rodney Harrison's blitz forced McNair to throw up a jump ball to Bennett, who bobbled it and had it knocked away by Asante Samuel.

"It was everything we expected of this game," Belichick said. "All their key players played well. We were fortunate to make more plays than Tennessee did."

"It was one of the more intense games I've played in," Harrison said.

The Patriots gained 297 yards to the Titans' 284. McNair played like a co-MVP, completing 18 of 26 passes for 210 yards. But, as it has all season, New England's defense stiffened when it had to. "It was our season," Harrison said. "We had let them go downfield, and enough was enough. We challenged them. We stepped up and said if they're going to beat us, they're going to beat us. You can't let him sit back there and sling the ball. We de-

After a brief celebration, Rodney Harrison mouthed the team mantra: one game at a time.

cided to try something different and give him a different look."

After the game the Patriots did not have the look of a team that was a win away from the Super Bowl. "We're not jumping for joy in here," Tedy Bruschi said. "We know what we want to do. We're just one step closer."

"We're not looking at the Super Bowl. We're looking at one game at a time," said Harrison, repeating what has become a familiar refrain. "You don't see guys jumping around. We're focused."

Titans guard Zach Piller was not impressed, even after the Patriots had beaten the Titans for a second time this season. "Everyone was talking about their defense," Piller said. "I thought it sucked. It'd be a shock to me if they were holding the trophy at the end of all of this... I will not leave this stadium thinking we got beat by a better team. I think that that team is not a very good team and it sickens me that we lost to them. It just wasn't our day."

The Titans took their first possession of the second half and marched

Tedy Bruschi's play lived up to the fans' billing as the Patriots advanced to the AFC title game.

70 yards in 11 plays, tying the game on McNair's 11-yard collaboration with Derrick Mason. The drive took 7:47 and included a 30-yard completion from McNair to Tyrone Calico. On the touchdown, Mason took McNair's short pass, slipped the attempted tackle of Asante Samuel, and leaped over Tyrone Poole and the pylon.

New England hadn't committed any major errors until tight end Daniel Graham fumbled (Kevin Carter forced it) and the Titans' Carlos Hall recovered near midfield. But the Patriots' defense didn't budge, forcing Tennessee into a three and out. Credit Willie McGinest for the stop; he blew up an attempted screen to Frank Wycheck, tackling the tight end for a 10-yard loss on first down.

That set the stage for the fourth quarter and more heroics from Vinatieri and the defense.

WINNING STRIDE

David Givens hails the Gillette Stadium crowd after they watched the Patriots deliver their 13th straight victory.

Jarvis Green completed a takedown of Peyton Manning for one of his three sacks.

Colts

Something had to give... and give

24 - 14

IND	0	0	7	7
NE	7	8	6	3

FOXBOROUGH

There's your answer, exclamation point included.

Oh, yes. The question. All week we wondered which would give in a clash between one of the more potent offenses in recent memory, that of the Indianapolis Colts, or a New England Patriots defense that can make itself comfortable in any discussion of dominant defenses. We got our answer. It was the Colts who gave in the AFC Championship game at Gillette

game with a postseason rating of 156.9 (a perfect QB rating is 158.3). Manning's rating yesterday: 35.5.

New England, which allowed only 68 points at home during the regular season (an eight-game record) and 36 in its previous seven home games, ran its record against MVPs this season to 4-0. The Patriots overcame both Manning and co-MVP Steve McNair twice en route to their second Super Bowl in three seasons, third since 1996, and fourth in franchise history.

Indianapolis averaged nearly 40 points in its first two postseason games. New England led, 15-0, at half-time and protected its lead in the second half.

The Patriots ran their winning-streak to 14 games and their home record to 10-0. They lived up to their motto. They protected their house.

"I thought Peyton deserved the attention he got. He was just downright hot," Tedy Bruschi said. "We looked at ourselves and saw some of the things that were being done defensively against them the previous two weeks

game at 7, and, in the second quarter, Law made a diving, one-handed catch of a pass intended for Marvin Harrison.

What kind of day was it for the Colts' offense? One fact says it all. Law and Marvin Harrison each caught the same number of Manning passes: three. The Patriots rushed only four men yet sacked Manning four times, three by Jarvis Green. That left seven defenders in coverage.

The Colts never got off and running on the wet, snowy Gillette field. With 4 minutes 13 seconds to go before half-time, Hunter Smith came on to punt for the first time in the postseason. Indianapolis couldn't even do that right. Long snapper Justin Snow sent it over Smith's head, and Smith kicked it out of his end zone for a safety and a 15-0 New England lead.

But the Colts had a chance to get back in it before the end of the half. They recovered Bethel Johnson's fumble, and drove to New England's 22-yard line, but Rodney Harrison forced a fumble by Marvin Harrison, and

What kind of day was it for the Colts' offense? One fact says it all. Ty Law and Marvin Harrison each caught the same number of Manning passes: three.

Stadium. They gave. And gave. And gave. And gave. And gave.

The Patriots won their fourth conference title yesterday and earned a trip to Super Bowl XXXVIII in Houston against the Carolina Panthers by intercepting league co-MVP Peyton Manning four times — three by Ty Law — and forcing five turnovers in a 24-14 victory. Manning came into the

and we thought, 'There's no way that's happening when they come in here.' We know what to do against this team. We're a physical ball club and they're finesse, so something had to give."

Manning gave the ball away to end the Colts' first two possessions. Rodney Harrison picked him off in the end zone in the first quarter with Indianapolis 5 yards from tying the

Tyrone Poole recovered.

The play was reminiscent of Antwan Harris's hit on the Rams' Ricky Proehl (now a Panther) that forced a fumble in the Super Bowl two years ago. Fitting, considering the Patriots viewed these Colts just as they did those Rams: soft.

"Bloody their nose up a little bit," Willie McGinest said. "Every play, make contact with the receivers, the tight ends, the backs, whoever."

"This was probably the most simple game plan that we had — just go out there and stick them and beat them up at the line of scrimmage," Law said. "If you watch those guys all through the season and postseason when they put up those big numbers, you see a lot of guys run through the secondary. We said we're not going to let them do

his usual efficient self, completing 22 of 37 passes for 237 yards, with 1 touchdown and 1 interception (his first at home this season). Adam Vinatieri kicked an AFC title game record-tying five field goals.

The Patriots even outgained the Colts, 349-306. Even New England's offensive players had had enough of all the talk about how dynamic the Colts were. "I just got sick and tired of hear-

Indianapolis turned the ball over five times, including four interceptions, and bumbled a punt attempt into a safety.

that to us, we're going to challenge them more so than other teams, and may the best man win.

"The only thing that you can beat speed with is power, and that's what we did."

The Patriots are a prideful bunch. They didn't take kindly to all the praise that was heaped upon Manning and Co. all week.

"They were so hot, they were blazing," Rodney Harrison said. "Coming in, nobody gave us a chance. One guy cannot win a championship. This is the ultimate team sport. It really gave us motivation and it really fueled the fire. We got tired of it. We give him all the credit in the world. He's a great quarterback. But one guy can't win it. It takes a team, and that's what we are."

Oh, yes. The offense. Antowain Smith gained 100 yards on 22 carries, and MVP runner-up Tom Brady was

ing about Peyton Manning and the Colts and the offense and they put up this many points," said Troy Brown (7 catches, 88 yards). "It was driving me nuts. Everybody in this locker room was tired of hearing about the Colts."

"We have a good offense," said David Givens, who scored the Patriots' only touchdown on a 7-yard pass from Brady. "A lot of people don't respect us, but if you watch the game, you'll see what we can do. Obviously we didn't take advantage of our red-zone opportunities, but we can move the ball."

And so it's on to the Panthers. Another win would be the Patriots' 15th in a row, and second championship in three years. As usual after posting a victory, the Patriots had a bigger objective in mind.

"AFC champs is one thing," Richard Seymour said, "but NFL champs is what we're really after." ✐

Antowain Smith, who had an even 100 yards against the Colts, busts through the line for a big gain.

THREE SACKS, AFTER HAVING JUST TWO ALL SEASON; THE PATRIOTS' SAFETY WAS THE FIRST IN TEAM PLAYOFF HISTORY

OUR HOUSE

Tom Brady, joined by wide receiver David Givens, was having a ball after the final gun sounded on the Patriots' second AFC championship in three years.

One more time

BY DAN SHAUGHNESSY

SUPER BOWL XXXVIII

Panthers

Brady, Vinatieri come through again

32 - 29

CAR	0	10	0	19
NE	0	14	0	18

HOUSTON

Yogi Berra would have called it, "Deja vu all over again."

It was all so familiar... Adam Vinatieri kicking the game-winner... quarterback Tom Brady winning the Most Valuable Player Award... coach Bill Belichick and owner Bob Kraft hoisting the Vince Lombardi Trophy while Patriot players hugged and brushed confetti off one another. All of these things happened two years ago when the Patriots upset the St. Louis Rams in New Orleans.

After the Patriots had beaten Carolina, 32-29, in Houston for their second Super Bowl in three years,

Kraft told the crowd, "Fifty-three players, 17 coaches, a head coach — the heart and soul of our team showed us what the concept of team is all about."

Championships are like children — you love each one equally. But the manner in which the 2003-04 Patriots went about their business makes this title a slightly favored son. The Patriots finished the season with 15 consecutive wins, went 10-0 against winning teams, and went 10 weeks without trailing in a game before the Panthers put them on the ropes at Reliant Stadium.

As ever, Brady was Joe Montana-cool under pressure. With the game tied and a little more than a minute to play, he moved the Patriots 37 yards in six plays, setting up Vinatieri's 41-yard kick for the win with four seconds left. The clutch kicker had missed a 31-yard chip shot, and had another attempt blocked, but his final boot was straight and true.

"Maybe a little deja vu of two years ago," said Vinatieri. "The fellows

moved the ball downfield and we had the opportunity to win it again. This never gets old. With this type of venue and the pressure on, it's never easy, but you try to block all the external things out and kick it. I'll cherish this for a long time."

Meanwhile, what's left for Brady? John Kerry's running mate? First man on Mars? Starting pitcher for the Red Sox when they finally win a World Series? The 26-year-old golden child becomes the youngest two-time Super Bowl-winning quarterback and one of only four players to win the MVP Award twice.

He completed 32 of 48 passes for 354 yards and three touchdowns. He is 6-0 lifetime in playoff games.

"The guys made some great catches there on that last drive," said Brady. "And Adam drove that sucker right down the middle to win it. What a game. Fitting for the Super Bowl, I guess."

When the Patriots trailed for the first time since before Thanksgiving,

It was deja vu all over again as New England knocked off the Cinderella Carolina Panthers courtesy of Adam Vinatieri's 41-yard field goal with four seconds left.

POSSESSION OF THE BALL FOR 38:58, CAROLINA HAS POSSESSION FOR 21:02; MIKE VRABEL (2), RODNEY HARRISON,

AND WILLIE MCGINEST COMBINE FOR FOUR SACKS, TOM BRADY IS NOT SACKED; BRADY'S 32 COMPLETIONS SET A SUPER

Tom Brady has Antowain Smith in his sights on the way to another Super Bowl MVP effort.

Brady moved them 68 yards in 11 plays and regained the lead with a 1-yard touchdown pass to linebacker Mike Vrabel. When the Panthers roared back to tie the game, Brady responded again.

"It was an awesome year," said Belichick. "I can't say enough about the players. We finished the game with two backup safeties. That's the way it's been all year."

So now it's Groundhog Day, where the scene keeps repeating itself, much like in the Bill Murray movie, but into the books as one of the best and most beloved Boston sports teams of the last 100 years. Not since the Larry Bird Celtics of 1984 and '86 has a local team won two championships in three seasons. The Bruins last did it in 1970 and '72 and the Red Sox haven't turned the trick since 1916 and '18.

The 2003-04 Patriots featured one of the best defenses in league history, used 42 different starters, had only two Pro Bowlers, and took pride in selflessness and interchangeable parts. At times, it looked as if they had 11

Time to put Tom Brady's handsome face on Boston's professional sports Mount Rushmore monument.

there's no one left to beat. Too bad. Patriots fans surely would embrace six more weeks of football. In the wake of the coldest January since 1888, and the most disappointing Red Sox finish since 1986, New England needed a lift, and the Patriots delivered with a season for the ages.

In the end, the Super Bowl win was like so many others in this magical Patriots season. The Patriots failed to overwhelm their opponents, relied on strong defense, got contributions from the entire roster, and left it to Brady and Vinatieri to come through at the finish. The fact that New England's final touchdown pass was caught by a linebacker tells you much of what you need to know about this team.

By any measure, these Patriots go coaches on the field. They transformed their two-year-old stadium into the happiest place on earth.

The camaraderie of the Patriots was evident at the start again. Troy Brown, the senior Patriot in continuous service, led the AFC champions onto the field. And as they did two years ago, the Patriots poured out of their tunnel en masse — a show of unity that was copied by the Panthers. It was clear at this moment that the Super Bowl would be like another home game for Belichick's team. Patriot Nation made its presence felt and there were moments when Reliant Stadium sounded like the football theater off Route 1 in Foxborough.

It started out like a World Cup game and was still 0-0 with a little more than three minutes to play in the first half. But Brady threw a pair of touchdown passes in the final three minutes and Carolina's Jake Delhomme started to move his team and New England led, 14-10, at intermission.

After a ribald halftime show featuring Janet Jackson, play was interrupted briefly when a streaker managed to line up with the Panthers for the opening kickoff. He was chased by authorities and eventually brought down when Pats linebacker Matt Chatham put a shoulder into him. Needless to say, Belichick was not amused.

It got wild again after a scoreless third quarter. The teams traded touchdowns early in the fourth. After a Brady interception, the Panthers struck again on the longest play from scrimmage in Super Bowl history, an 85-yard pass from Delhomme to Muhsin Muhammad. Carolina led, 22-21, with 6:53 left.

Brady went to work and it was madness the rest of the way. As always, the Patriots came through in the clutch.

No doubt there will be whispers of "dynasty." The well-managed, brilliantly coached Patriots are in position to make it back to the national stage in Jacksonville next year. ✎

PATRIOTS' SUPER BOWL WINS; ADAM VINATIERI MISSES THE FIRST TWO FIELD GOALS BUT HITS THE GAME WINNER, JUST

Adam Vinatieri stands alone after sending the scrappy Panthers home as losers.

SEA OF JOY

Rodney Harrison, his arm in a sling, soaks in his first championship with the Patriots.

"Bingo, we win again!"

The Patriots hardly could have done more to captivate New Englanders in 2003, running off 15 consecutive wins and returning home with their second championship in three years.

JUST DUCKY

More than 1.5 million fans saluted the Patriots
as they boarded duck boats and rolled through
downtown Boston with the Super Bowl trophy.
Troy Brown, Tedy Bruschi, Larry Izzo and Tom
Brady delivered the hardware to City Hall Plaza.

2003 ROSTER

#	NAME	POS	HT	WT	AGE	YR	WHEN/HOW ACQUIRED	COLLEGE
4	Adam Vinatieri	K	6'0"	202	31	8	1996 free agent	South Dakota State
6	Rohan Davey	QB	6'2"	245	25	2	2004 Draft—4th Round	Louisiana State
12	Tom Brady	QB	6'4"	225	26	4	2000 Draft—6th Round	Michigan
13	Ken Walter	P	6'1"	207	31	7	2001 free agent	Kent State
17	Dedric Ward	WR	5'9"	187	29	7	2003 free agent (BAL)	Northern Iowa
19	Damon Huard	QB	6'3"	215	30	7	2001 free agent (MIA)	Washington
21	Michael Cloud	RB	5'10"	205	28	5	2003 free agent (KC)	Boston College
22	Asante Samuel	CB	5'10"	185	22	R	2003 Draft—4th Round	Central Florida
23	Antwan Harris	DB	5'9"	194	26	4	2000 Draft—6th Round	Virginia
24	Ty Law	CB	5'11"	200	29	9	1995 Draft—1st Round	Michigan
26	Eugene Wilson	DB	5'10"	195	23	R	2003 Draft—2nd Round	Illinois
30	Je'Rod Cherry	S	6'1"	210	30	8	2001 free agent	California
31	Larry Centers	FB	6'0"	225	35	14	2003 free agent (BUF)	Stephen F. Austin
32	**Antowain Smith**	**RB**	**6'2"**	**232**	**31**	**7**	**2001 free agent (BUF)**	**Houston**
33	Kevin Faulk	RB	5'8"	202	27	5	1999 Draft—2nd Round	Louisiana State
34	Chris Akins	S	5'11"	200	27	5	2003 free agent (CLE)	Arkansas-Pine Bluff
35	Patrick Pass	FB	5'10"	217	26	4	2000 Draft—7th Round	Georgia
37	**Rodney Harrison**	**S**	**6'1"**	**220**	**31**	**10**	**2003 free agent (SD)**	**Western Illinois**
38	Tyrone Poole	CB	5'8"	188	31	8	2003 free agent (DEN)	Fort Valley State
39	Shawn Mayer	S	6'0"	202	24	R	2003 free agent	Penn State
46	Brian Kinchen	LS	6'2"	240	38	14	2003 free agent (CAR)	Louisiana State
48	Tully Banta-Cain	LB	6'2"	250	23	R	2003 Draft—7th Round	California
50	Mike Vrabel	LB	6'4"	261	28	7	2001 free agent (PIT)	Ohio State
51	Don Davis	LB	6'1"	235	31	8	2003 free agent (STL)	Kansas
52	Ted Johnson	LB	6'4"	253	31	9	1995 Draft—2nd Round	Colorado
53	Larry Izzo	LB	5'10"	228	29	8	2001 free agent (MIA)	Rice
54	Tedy Bruschi	LB	6'1"	247	30	8	1996 Draft—3rd Round	Arizona
55	Willie McGinest	LB	6'5"	270	32	10	1994 Draft'1st Round	Southern Cal
58	Matt Chatham	LB	6'4"	250	26	4	2000 Waivers (STL)	South Dakota
60	Wilbert Brown	G	6'2"	320	26	3	2003 Waivers (WAS)	Houston
63	Joe Andruzzi	G	6'3"	312	28	7	2000 free agent	Southern Connecticut St.
65	Damien Woody	C/G	6'3"	320	26	5	1999 Draft—1st Round	Boston College
67	Dan Koppen	C	6'2"	296	24	R	2003 Draft—5th Round	Boston College
68	Tom Ashworth	T	6'6"	305	26	2	2001 free agent	Colorado
71	Russ Hochstein	G	6'4"	305	26	3	2003 free agent	Nebraska
72	Matt Light	T	6'4"	305	25	3	2001 Draft—2nd Round	Purdue
76	Brandon Gorin	T	6'6"	308	25	2	2003 free agent	Purdue
80	**Troy Brown**	**WR**	**5'10"**	**196**	**32**	**11**	**1993 Draft—8th round**	**Marshall**

#	NAME	POS	HT	WT	AGE	YR	WHEN/HOW ACQUIRED	COLLEGE
81	Bethel Johnson	WR	5'11"	200	24	R	2003 Draft—2nd round	Texas A&M
82	Daniel Graham	TE	6'3"	257	25	2	2002 Draft—1st Round	Colorado
83	**Deion Branch**	**WR**	**5'9"**	**193**	**24**	**2**	**2002 Draft—2nd Round**	**Louisville**
84	Fred Baxter	TE	6'3"	268	32	11	2002 free agent (CHI)	Auburn
87	David Givens	WR	6'0"	212	23	2	2002 Draft—7th Round	Notre Dame
88	Christian Fauria	TE	6'4"	250	32	9	2002 free agent (SEA)	Colorado
90	Dan Klecko	DL	5'11"	283	22	R	2003 Draft—4th Round	Temple
91	Bobby Hamilton	DE	6'5"	280	32	9	2000 free agent (NYJ)	Southern Mississippi
92	Ted Washington	NT	6'5"	365	35	13	2003 Trade (CHI)	Louisville
93	Richard Seymour	DL	6'6"	310	24	3	2001 Draft—1st Round	Georgia
94	Ty Warren	DL	6'5"	300	22	R	2003 Draft—1st Round	Texas A&M
95	**Roman Phifer**	**LB**	**6'2"**	**248**	**35**	**13**	**2001 free agent (NYJ)**	**UCLA**
96	Rick Lyle	DL	6'5"	285	32	10	2002 free agent (NYJ)	Missouri
97	Jarvis Green	DL	6'3"	290	24	2	2002 Draft—4th Round	Louisiana State
98	Anthony Pleasant	DE	6'5"	280	35	14	2001 free agent (SF)	Tennessee State

RESERVE LIST / INJURED

#	NAME	POS	HT	WT	AGE	YR	WHEN/HOW ACQUIRED	COLLEGE
59	Rosevelt Colvin	LB	6'3"	250	26	5	2003 free agent (CHI)	Purdue
77	Mike Compton	G/C	6'6"	310	33	11	2001 free agent (DET)	West Virginia
16	Kliff Kingsbury	QB	6'3"	220	24	R	2003 Draft—6th Round	Texas Tech
70	Adrian Klemm	T	6'3"	312	26	4	2000 Draft—2nd Round	Hawaii
44	Fred McCrary	FB	6'0"	247	30	7	2003 free agent (SD)	Mississippi State
49	Sean McDermott	LS	6'4"	250	27	3	2003 free agent (MIA)	Kansas
64	Gene Mruczkowski	OL	6'2"	305	23	R	2003 free agent	Purdue
61	Stephen Neal	G	6'4"	305	27	2	2001 free agent	Cal State-Bakersfield
86	David Patten	WR	5'10"	190	29	7	2001 free agent (CLE)	Western Carolina
66	Lonie Paxton	LS	6'2"	260	25	4	2000 free agent	Sacramento State

COACHES

HEAD COACH Bill Belichick

ASSISTANTS: DEFENSIVE COORDINATOR & DEFENSIVE LINE Romeo Crennel

OFFENSIVE COORDINATOR Charlie Weis / STRENGTH & CONDITIONING Mike Woicik

WIDE RECEIVERS Brian Daboll / ASSISTANT OFFENSIVE LINE & TIGHT ENDS Jeff Davidson

RUNNING BACKS Ivan Fears / QUARTERBACKS John Hufnagel / COACHING ASSISTANT Josh McDaniels

INSIDE LINEBACKERS Pepper Johnson / DEFENSIVE BACKS Eric Mangini

ASSISTANT STRENGTH & CONDITIONING Markus Paul / OUTSIDE LINEBACKERS Rob Ryan

ASSISTANT HEAD COACH & OFFENSIVE LINE Dante Scarnecchia / SPECIAL TEAMS Brad Seely

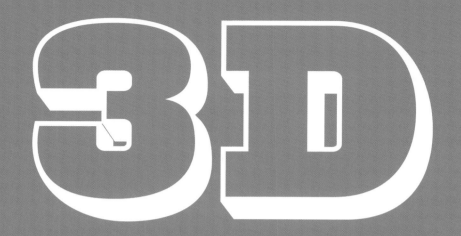

3D

DEFENSE, DEDICATION, DYNASTY

CHAPTER THREE

2004 predictions

They can't argue no one's giving them respect anymore. They're everybody's favorite. **RON BORGES**

Celtics were the last true dynasty. Don't know if Patriots can measure up. **NICK CAFARDO**

Post-title woes can't be avoided entirely. Just pray the QB's charmed life continues. **BOB RYAN**

Hard part is picking four losses. Best Boston franchise since '60s Celtics. **DAN SHAUGHNESSY**

But if they trade Nomar, it's 16-0 because that seems to do the trick. **JIM McCABE**

FINAL 14-2

Indianapolis Colts
Arizona Cardinals
Buffalo Bills
Miami Dolphins
Seattle Seahawks
New York Jets
Pittsburgh Steelers
St. Louis Rams
Buffalo Bills
Kansas City Chiefs
Baltimore Ravens
Cleveland Browns
Cincinnati Bengals
Miami Dolphins
New York Jets
San Francisco 49ers

Postseason

Indianapolis Colts
Pittsburgh Steelers
Philadelphia Eagles

2 0 0

04

Colts

Defensive plays make difference

27 - 24

IND	0	17	0	7
NE	3	10	14	0

FOXBOROUGH

In the end, you could argue that the only team that could stop the Indianapolis Colts was the Indianapolis Colts, but then you wouldn't be giving due credit to two incredible defensive plays by Eugene Wilson and Willie McGinest.

As hard as Edgerrin James ran in the season opener, he coughed up the football twice when the Colts had chances to score, none more critical than at the Patriots' 1-yard line late in the fourth quarter. As James put his head down and ran straight ahead, Wilson poked the ball out, and rookie Vince Wilfork recovered to preserve the Patriots' 27-24 win.

It extended the Patriots' win streak to 16 games, two short of the NFL record, and it certainly wasn't easy. The Patriots trailed, 17-13, at halftime in a game that featured superb offensive performances by Tom Brady (26 of 38, 335 yards, three touchdowns), David Patten, and Corey Dillon.

Trailing, 27-17, after three quarters, the Colts began their comeback, taking advantage of Ty Law's injury as Tyrone Poole and Asante Samuel were the cornerbacks covering the Colts' dangerous receivers. Poole and Mike Vrabel were flagged for interfering with receivers, and Law, who implored coach Bill Belichick to let him back in the game, finally was allowed to re-

turn, only to give up a 7-yard touchdown pass from Peyton Manning to Brandon Stokley to make it 27-24 with 11:05 remaining.

The Patriots made two consecutive mistakes — a Brady interception by Nick Harper and a Deion Branch muff of a punt, which gave the Colts great field position and set up James's goal-line fumble. The Colts then foiled the Patriots' attempt to run out the clock, and when Manning found Stokley for a 45-yard completion, the Colts were deep in New England territory. After a crushing 12-yard sack by McGinest, Mike Vanderjagt missed a 48-yard field goal wide right with 24 seconds remaining.

Predictably, offensive coordinator Charlie Weis had the Patriots come out passing the ball against a young and depleted Colts secondary. Brady completed passes of 19 yards (to David Givens), 14 (to Branch), and 14 (to Ben Watson) as the Patriots quickly found themselves at the Colts' 10-yard line, before a delay-of-game penalty forced them to settle for Adam Vinatieri's 32-yard field goal.

The Colts responded with an impressive drive of their own, starting at their 28 and moving to the Patriots' 6. The big play was a 42-yard hookup from Manning to Reggie Wayne, who was lined up in the slot against Vrabel and easily beat the linebacker down the field. The Colts were running effectively with James between the tackles, but just when you thought they would stick with what was working, Manning dropped back to pass.

Ty Warren got strong pressure up the middle and forced Manning to throw into a crowd of Patriot jerseys near the goal line. Tedy Bruschi came up with the interception, foiling the Colts' chance to tie or take the lead.

On the Colts' next series, Manning connected with James for 6 yards,

Marvin Harrison for 9, and James for 20 to the Patriots' 29. The Colts advanced as far as the 14, but Manning's third-down pass to Harrison in the end zone was broken up by Wilson. Vanderjagt came on to make his 42d consecutive field goal, from 32 yards with 13:44 remaining in the second quarter. ✏

Cardinals

17th straight not an artistic success

23 - 12

NE	7	7	3	6
AZ	0	6	6	0

TEMPE, ARIZ.

One of these days a rising team like the Arizona Cardinals is going to come out of the blue and beat the defending Super Bowl champions, but this wasn't going to be the day.

The Cardinals might have been pesky and tough, the 100-degree heat on the field posed some problems, and the emotional halftime tribute to Pat Tillman gave the Patriots all they could handle, but New England has made winning a habit and an art form.

The Patriots probably should have given the Cardinals a thumping, but still extended their winning streak to 17 with a 23-12 triumph over the Cardinals before a crowd of 51,557.

The Patriots had the majority of the crowd behind them in what was a quasi home game, and they certainly had all the sexy statistics in their favor, including Corey Dillon's 158 yards on 32 carries, and David Givens's 118 receiving yards on six catches. The Cardinals'

ted negative yardage, and only two drives were more than 40 yards in length as New England held Arizona to one touchdown.

"I have to say congratulations to Bill Belichick and his team," said Cardinals coach Dennis Green. "Winning 17 games in a row is absolutely incredible. It was a very physical football game."

The win, which was followed by a week off, wasn't good enough for some of the Patriots, especially not quarterback Tom Brady, who threw two touchdown passes to Daniel Graham but also threw two interceptions.

"We left a lot of plays out there and we have stuff we're going to have to correct," Brady said. "I think the way we're playing is not going to be good enough much longer."

The day wasn't that easy for the 2-0 Patriots, but it was never that difficult, either.

"We just wanted to be aggressive, come after them hard, make their quarterback make some tough reads, and stop the run," said Patriots defensive lineman Richard Seymour, who was a stalwart on the three-man line along with Vince Wilfork and Ty Warren, who were rotated with Keith Traylor and Jarvis Green later on.

The Cardinals (0-2) mounted their best drive of the game for almost eight minutes of the third quarter, going 80 yards after Adam Vinatieri had hit a 29-yard field goal, one of his three on the day.

After Ty Law was called for pass interference on Bryant Johnson in the end zone, placing the ball at the 1, Emmitt Smith powered in to cut the gap to 5 points, 17-12. The Cardinals went for 2, and couldn't take advan-

Josh McCown was sacked five times in the first half while being held to a 33.7 quarterback rating, and the Patriots defense held the Cardinals to 167 total yards, only 50 net yards rushing.

The defense was out there for 11 Cardinals possessions. Four of them were three-and-out, two of them net-

tage of the Patriots having only 10 men on the field as McCown had a receiver open in the end zone and never saw him.

As it turned out, the Law penalty didn't haunt the Patriots as the defense tightened up and forced the Cardinals into consecutive three-and-outs in the fourth quarter. ✐

Bills

Big defensive play again turns the tide

31-17

NE	10	7	0	14
BUF	10	7	0	0

ORCHARD PARK, NY Tom Brady walked out of the Patriots locker room to the podium in the interview room at Ralph Wilson Stadium smiling, and why not? Though he's not supposed to think about it, the team he quarterbacks had just won its 18th straight game, a 31-17 triumph over the Bills, tying the record for the most consecutive wins including postseason games.

In some locker rooms that would have been cause for champagne streaming through the air, a celebration of a remarkable record that, with one more victory, would be all theirs. Miami also won 18 straight including postseason, in 1972 and '73, including an undefeated '72 season.

But in New England's locker room, the only thing the players were doing while getting dressed was trying to dodge the media and questions about the streak.

"Better standing up here now than last year [after a 31-0 loss]," Brady

joked. "We had a lot of penalties and missed opportunities, but we settled in in the second half. They have a very good team."

Once again, when it really counted, in a game that was tied at 17 and anyone's to win for three-plus quarters, the Patriots seized the moment. In the end they played like Super Bowl champions; the Bills played like a team in disarray and likely heading for some major changes, perhaps even the unseating of Drew Bledsoe at quarterback.

The Patriots were confident if it came down to the end, they could rattle Bledsoe. While they spared him most of the game, they blitzed him into oblivion in the fourth quarter. If they were banking on Bledsoe's teammates not being able to bail him out, they were right.

"We just wanted the ball to come out fast," said Patriots strong safety Rodney Harrison, who was relentless at the end. "Our front guys really did a wonderful job putting pressure on Drew. We didn't play very well in the first half, but in the second half we made some adjustments and we were able to pull out a very tough divisional win in a very tough place to play."

The game was iced with New England ahead, 24-17, late in the fourth quarter. The Bills drove to the Patriots' 17 where Bledsoe took a fourth-and-3 snap, faked a handoff to Travis Henry, and never saw Tedy Bruschi bearing down on him, unabated. Bruschi knocked the ball loose and Richard Seymour picked it up and lumbered 68 yards for the clinching score.

"I'm just glad I got into the end zone," Seymour said. "I'm not used to running that far, but you always like scoring touchdowns when you're a defensive player."

The Bills were running a bootleg for Bledsoe, believing it was a play the Patriots would least expect.

They were probably right, except it looked like Bledsoe was merely dropping back and starting to roll right before Henry allowed Bruschi to come clean and Bruschi knocked the ball loose.

Buffalo wide receiver Eric Moulds had a different take on the play.

"It was a situation where I think Travis went the wrong way," said Moulds. "Drew was supposed to hand it off to him, but Travis went the wrong way, and Drew never really got a chance to put the ball away. The guy hit him, made the play, and [they] scored." ✐

David Givens slips behind safety Coy Wire for a 44-yard gain to set up New England's first touchdown.

Dolphins

A record-breaker, not a show-stopper

24-10

MIA	0	7	3	0
NE	7	10	7	0

FOXBOROUGH
There was no champagne-spraying celebration in the Patriots locker room following their historic 24-10 victory over the Miami Dolphins. In fact, the only person who got wet was coach Bill Belichick, who received a Gatorade shower from Richard Seymour and Rodney Harrison in the final seconds.

A smiling Belichick acknowledged the crowd with waves to every side of the stadium, shook hands with most of his players for their part in the 19-game winning streak, including post-

season, gave out some attaboys, and then, according to Harrison, the coach said, "However, we have a great Seattle team coming in."

End of celebration.

The Dolphins really didn't defend the honor of the 1972 team, the only one to go undefeated in a season and one of the teams that had won 18 straight. In fact, Miami (0-5) is closer to becoming a winless team than it is to resembling its '72 forebears.

This wasn't one of the 19 straight that will be remembered as an artistic

Seattle's Ken Hamlin takes down Patriots tight end Daniel Graham.

success, and the Patriots haven't had one of those in their first four games. But they do enough to get the job done, and yesterday was no exception.

Down three receivers because of injuries to Troy Brown (shoulder) and Deion Branch (knee), and the benching of Bethel Johnson, and dealing with defensive injuries as well, including cornerback Tyrone Poole, the Patriots were playing reserves at key positions. At times one could see Dexter Reid at safety, Randall Gay (who had an interception) at corner, Kevin Kasper at receiver and kick returner, or Rabih Abdullah at tailback.

The Dolphins had their own problems, losing kicker Olindo Mare (right calf) before the opening kickoff, forcing punt returner Wes Welker to handle kickoff, extra point, and field goal duties. Welker, who had minimal kicking experience at Texas Tech, booted a 29-yard field goal and nailed an extra point. And late in the fourth quarter, the Dolphins lost two quarterbacks in three plays.

Starter Jay Fiedler suffered a rib injury on a 12-yard sack by Harrison. Two plays later, A.J. Feeley took a shot to his ribs on an incomplete pass to Chris Chambers on fourth and 7 and probably would not have come back had the Patriots not been able to run out the clock.

The New England defense made three exceptional red-zone stands in the fourth quarter.

"We just didn't want to give up those points," Harrison said. "It was just a matter of pride. Guys came up with plays, and time and time again that's the character of this team."

Cornerback Ty Law said he got himself motivated by all the hype

about the Miami defense during the week. Law said he didn't want to leave the game without feeling the Patriots' defense had outplayed Miami's.

"I'm playing against another corner [Sam Madison] over there, and I want to come out of it having the better game," said Law. ⃝

Seahawks

Chatter silenced, streak extended

30 - 20

SEA	0	6	3	11
NE	10	10	0	10

FOXBOROUGH

The Patriots won their 20th game in a row, and tied the NFL record for most consecutive regular-season wins (17). Those are feats that take all the emotion the players can muster week after week.

Each week there is a new cause to rally around. Next up would be a matchup against AFC East rival New York, also 5-0, but this week, Rodney Harrison took a few words from usually quiet Seattle receiver Darrell Jackson, who said among other things the Patriots were "beatable," and he turned them into what Harrison called "fuel for the fire."

"Two losses in a row [for the Seahawks]," Harrison said. "Breaks my heart."

The fiery Patriots safety, who had another strong game in the 30-20 win over the Seahawks at Gillette Stadium, said the team plays too hard to accept what he terms "disrespectful chatter" from the opposition. Harrison believes New England's opponents should re-

spect "a bunch of guys who work hard every week to prepare to play football as a team." He claimed he turned to Jackson at one point and said, "Why don't you just shut up and play?"

"We don't have a bunch of clowns in here," Harrison said. "We have good, quality people. It's a tough locker room if you're a prima donna. There's not one guy who singles himself out as being better or different than anyone else."

If wide receiver Bethel Johnson was in danger of becoming one of those guys, a trip to the Bill Belichick House of Detention seems to have rehabilitated him quickly. Johnson, who according to team sources was having problems executing the plays in the playbook, and was inactive for last week's game, made the catch of his life late in the fourth quarter. His full-extension, diving grab of a 48-yard pass from Tom Brady after outracing everyone in a Seahawk uniform kept alive New England's clinching drive.

"I guarantee that he is definitely the only guy on this team and probably one of the few guys in the league that could have caught up to that ball, because of his speed," said Patriots cornerback Ty Law.

The Seahawks' Josh Brown had just made a 31-yard field goal to trim the Patriots' advantage to 23-20 with 3:01 left. Brown, however, hit a bad kickoff to the 9, and Johnson ran it to the Patriot 37, from where New England started its clinching march.

Johnson's great grab came on third and 7 from the Patriot 40. The completion was challenged by Seahawks coach Mike Holmgren, but the call on the field was upheld. While the ball hit the ground with Johnson's arms wrapped around it, the ruling was that the receiver had held on. The play appeared to break the spirits of the Seahawks, who two plays later allowed a 9-yard touchdown run by Corey

Dillon, who controlled the clock for the Patriots all day with 105 yards and two touchdowns on 23 carries.

"I think he made a great catch," Holmgren said of Johnson's acrobatics. "I saw the play differently from the referee, but any way you look at it, it was a great effort by a great athlete. But, you know what, that is what this team has been able to do. It's a remarkable thing. You tip your hat to them." ⃝

Jets

Record pales before key divisional win

13 - 7

NYJ	0	7	0	0
NE	3	10	0	0

FOXBOROUGH

As the newspaper of record, we must inform our readers that the 13-7 Patriots win over the New York Jets in Game 6 broke the NFL record for consecutive regular-season victories. The team has 18, 21 overall.

We also had to inform the participants. "Is that right?" said Patriots wide receiver David Patten, who caught what held up as the winning touchdown pass from Tom Brady from 7 yards out with five seconds remaining in the first half. "I didn't know that. It is what it is. It's a sign we've done a great job to this point, but we have two-thirds of the season to play."

Coach Bill Belichick said that neither before nor after the defensive struggle did he mention the NFL record. In fact, he said, "[I] didn't say one word about it." What meant more than the amazing streak of excellence

2001

Tom Brady is the team's leading passer. Drew Bledsoe had held that spot for the previous eight seasons.

2003
Tom Brady had three touchdowns passes of 50 yards or more.

2004
Tom Brady had a career-high QB rating of 92.6 and tied his career high for TD passes in a season with 28.

with 32 against the Panthers in Super Bowl XXXVIII.

After 21 consecutive victories, the Patriots and quarterback Tom Brady were out of answers.

was that the Patriots took sole possession of first place in the AFC East by beating their divisional rivals, a team that wasn't quite ready to knock the dynasty-in-the-making off its game.

It was another instance of the Patriots (6-0) doing what they had to do at the most opportune time, just as in so many of their other wins. A team that hates to mention individual accolades got 115 yards on 22 carries from Corey Dillon; five receptions for 107 yards from David Givens, who shouldered the load with Deion Branch and Troy Brown out with injuries; and a 20-for-29 (for 230 yards and one TD) performance from Brady, who had a gaudy 104.1 quarterback rating. New England also gave tremendous effort on defense, holding the Jets to 268 total yards of offense and Curtis Martin to 70 yards on 20 carries.

And like most games during the streak, the opposition had a chance to overtake the Patriots at one time or another. When that time comes, the Patriots, who have asserted themselves as the best late-game team in football, usually make a huge stop or break the opposing team's rhythm.

Such a play occurred on third and 5 from the Patriots' 27 with 2:48 remaining when Martin ran his patented draw play and the Patriots were ready to seize the moment once more.

Richard Seymour pushed the pocket from the right end. Willie McGinest came from the back side and once again made one of his amazing stops, a la the one he made against Indianapolis last season, or the one against Tennessee. He nailed Martin for a 3-yard loss, the same Martin who Belichick said during the week never makes negative plays. Until that moment, he had not.

"In that situation, you have to play the run first," McGinest said. "I had my half and Richard had his half and we came together and made a play."

It wasn't the final play for the Jets (5-1), either, but the Patriots took care of that as well. On fourth and 8, Chad Pennington threw downfield to Wayne Chrebet. The veteran slot receiver was covered well all day by free agent rookie Randall Gay, and he once again was all over Chrebet. The Patriots figured Pennington would look for Chrebet on such an important throw and Rodney Harrison came over to break up the play, preserving the victory.

The Patriots have concentration, maturity, "and we don't panic," Harrison said. "We go through a lot of situational football, so when it is a critical moment, we don't panic. Someone always steps up and makes a play." ⬭

Steelers

A good thing comes to an end

20 - 34

NE	3	7	3	7
PIT	21	3	10	0

PITTSBURGH

Their baseball brothers, the Red Sox, are proof that all streaks must end, winning the World Series after an 86-year drought. So as if to balance the slate, the sports gods looked down upon New England and said, "Do not be greedy."

Thus, the Patriots' record 21-game winning streak ended. The Team That Could Not Lose finally met its match in the Pittsburgh Steelers, 34-20, before a record-breaking Heinz Field crowd of 64,737.

There were no excuses from anyone in the Patriots locker room as to why they lost for the first time since Sept. 28, 2003, to the Steve Spurrier-coached Washington Redskins.

That's because the Steelers played very much in their tradition, dominating the trenches, creating mistakes, and smashing Patriots quarterback Tom Brady in the mouth every chance they got.

"I wish we could play again tomorrow," said New England defensive end Willie McGinest. "We're not going to make any excuses, like blame the refs, or injuries, or anything like that. It's disappointing we got our butts kicked and got outplayed. We have to come in tomorrow and look in the mirror and make sure each and every one of us can see what we did to add to this. It's not the end of the world. We have time to come back from this."

The Steelers forced turnovers — four of them — all of which led to Pittsburgh scores. Two were caused by linebacker Jerry Porter, who played an emotional game, saying he was fired up by words McGinest uttered to him before the opening kickoff.

If that was the case, he made the Pats pay big time, and young quarterback Ben Roethlisberger (18 for 24 for 196 yards, two touchdowns and a 126.4 rating) looked as calm and collected as a guy named Bradshaw in picking apart the wounded Patriots secondary.

They didn't make excuses, but the Patriots were missing starting running back Corey Dillon, had to use a makeshift offensive line with starting right tackle Tom Ashworth out with a back ailment, and then lost left tackle Matt Light, who got the wind knocked out of him.

The Patriots also lost cornerback Ty Law to a foot injury in the third series of the game, and the Steelers went right at rookie free agent Randall Gay and made the Patriots pay.

But in the past, the Patriots had never missed a beat because of injuries.

"We've lost players to injuries

Rodney Harrison, right, salutes Roman Phifer after Phifer picked off a St. Louis pass.

before," said linebacker Tedy Bruschi. "We play as a team. Whoever is in the game has to do their part. That's the way we do it around here."

With Dillon out, New England ran the ball six times for 5 yards, forcing Brady to throw it 43 times. The defense allowed the Steelers to romp for 221 yards on 49 carries, 125 of them from Duce Staley on 25 carries. Jerome Bettis, who ran for 65 more yards on 15 carries after totaling 64 yards in the first six games, was effective in the fourth quarter.

Time of possession was 42:58 to 17:02 in favor of the Steelers, who amassed 417 yards in total offense to the Patriots' 248.

Would things have been different if Dillon or Law had played?

"I couldn't forecast how [Dillon] was going to play," said Brady, who was picked off twice and sacked four times. "Corey's absence didn't force me into fumbling the ball." ⬭

Rams

Redoubled effort trumps adversity

40 - 22

NE	6	13	14	7
STL	0	14	0	8

ST. LOUIS

Over the last three years, the New England Patriots have defined the word "team." On this day, they redefined it and along the way embarrassed an ill-prepared team that couldn't execute, the St. Louis Rams, 40-22, at the Edward Jones Dome.

The Patriots had a linebacker catch a pass for a touchdown, a kicker throw a pass for a touchdown, and a wide receiver, practice squad player, linebacker, and rookie free agent all play defensive back at various times without serious consequences. It all symbolized what has made the Patriots the most resilient team in the league.

"This is probably as much of a team victory as anything I've ever been around," coach Bill Belichick said. "They fought to the end. That's what a team's about. Everyone doing their job."

With both starting cornerbacks and right tackle Tom Ashworth out before the opening kickoff, and reserve corner Asante Samuel knocked out for much of the day on the Rams' second play with a jammed shoulder, the Patriots were facing the kind of uphill battle to which Sisyphus could have related. But that ancient myth did not apply in the end, because the Patriots not only pushed their personal boulder up the hill, they then rolled it over the Rams.

Always, it seems, these Patriots play their best when the situation is at its worst, and it couldn't get much worse than having their secondary riddled by injury as they were facing one of the most explosive pass offenses in football.

Despite those problems, they left their opponent so bamboozled that after three quarters the Rams had attempted only 19 passes. If ever there was a game that cried out for abandoning a sense of balance, this was it. But St. Louis failed to take that course in part because the Patriots were hellbent on harassing their quarterback, sacking Marc Bulger five times and knocking him around on many other occasions.

Meanwhile, the Rams committed enough turnovers (three) and penalties (10) to beat themselves.

"I think it really came down to being more physical than they were," defensive end Richard Seymour said. "We wanted to pressure Bulger to get the ball out of there quick so they didn't have time to get into their routes."

New England's secondary problems were compounded on the second defensive play of the game when Samuel injured his right shoulder tackling tight end Brandon Manumaleuna. Samuel was replaced by wide receiver Troy Brown, who was involved in a tackle on running back Marshall Faulk on the very next play. Before the day was out, Brown would be the epitome of what the Patriots are about, catching a touchdown pass on a fake field goal, making three receptions, three tackles, and nearly intercepting two passes.

"The coaches were schooling me on the run," Brown said of his first NFL game as the Chuck Bednarik of his day, a two-way player in a time of specialists. "It was a little intimidating at first to be out there against some of the best guys to play wide receiver, but after I got a little sweat worked up I got more comfortable. That's what they teach you around here. Prepare for everything." ✎

Bills

Challenge fails to materialize

29 - 6

BUF	0	0	6	0
NE	3	17	3	6

FOXBOROUGH

If you listened to New England coach Bill Belichick and others speaking about the Bills coming into this game, Drew Bledsoe was playing like the second coming of Johnny Unitas, and Willis McGahee was running like Walter Payton.

At the conclusion of 60 minutes of football though, Bledsoe looked more like a 40-something George Blanda while McGahee looked like a running back with a bad leg.

By virtue of a 29-6 win over the Bills at Gillette Stadium, the Patriots kept pace with the Pittsburgh Steelers for the best record in the AFC at 8-1. They also went two games up on the New York Jets in the East Division.

The "new-look" Bills never materialized as the Patriots scorched them with touchdown passes by Tom Brady to David Patten for 13 yards and Christian Fauria for 5, Corey Dillon's fifth 100-yard rushing game (151 yards), and Adam Vinatieri's five field goals.

"We didn't play well enough to beat anybody," lamented Bills coach Mike Mularkey. "They don't make any mistakes. I felt like all week I got caught up in the fact that we felt good about

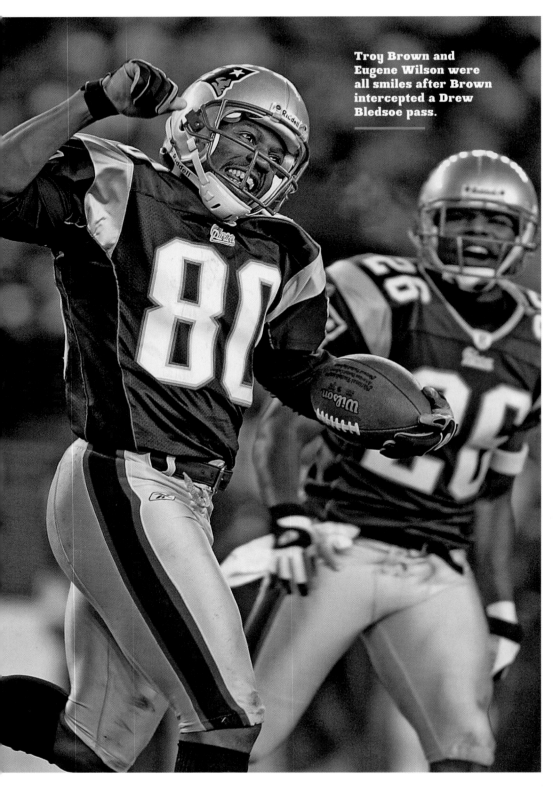

Troy Brown and Eugene Wilson were all smiles after Brown intercepted a Drew Bledsoe pass.

the week we had. The players were excited about it. I wish I had an answer. They challenged us to bring it at them and we didn't answer the call."

Bledsoe, 8 for 19 for 76 yards and a quarterback rating of 14.3 in one of his worst games as a pro, was continually pressured and forced into bad throws after the Patriots had stopped McGahee (14 carries for 37 yards) in his tracks.

Bledsoe was picked off three times, and the ultimate indignity was getting intercepted by Troy Brown in the fourth quarter on a pass intended for Eric Moulds.

"Eric Moulds was in the slot and he's their go-to guy," said Brown, who caught many passes from Bledsoe when he was the Patriots' QB. "I figured they'd be throwing it to him, so I was ready."

The only positive for the Bills, who had just eight first downs, converted no third downs in seven attempts, and were outgained in net yards, 428-125, was a 70-yard punt return in the third quarter by Jonathan Smith, which ruined New England's shutout bid.

Bledsoe was trying to shed the image that he can't play well against New England. He now has a 1-5 record against his former team.

Bledsoe has thrown 11 interceptions and five touchdown passes in games against Belichick's team. Brady is now 7-1 against Buffalo, throwing 14 touchdown passes and seven interceptions against the Bills.

While the Patriots settled for 3 points in their first two red-zone visits, they managed two touchdowns in their next two, taking a 20-0 halftime lead.

"It seemed as if we were dominating the game, but we'd only come up with 3 points," said Fauria. "We kept saying, 'We should be up by more than 6-0.'" ⊘

Chiefs

Battle is won in the trenches

27-19

NE	7	10	7	3
KC	10	0	3	6

KANSAS CITY

The sweat was dripping off Ted Johnson's face as if someone had forgotten to turn off a bathroom faucet. With each drop came the satisfaction that the Patriots' defense again had risen to the challenge, not only holding the NFL's No. 1 rushing team to 64 yards on the ground and surviving a patchwork secondary for one more week, but holding up in the fourth quarter, allowing the Pats to claim their ninth win in 10 games.

"Our defensive line did an unbelievable job," said Johnson following the 27-19 win over the Chiefs. "We didn't give up anything up the middle. To be a good defense, you have to stop the run. We knew we had to stop their run, and doing that we made them be a one-dimensional team — and that wasn't easy, either."

The Chiefs and their All-Pro offensive line fell far short in the battle of the trenches. Not only was Priest Holmes replacement Derrick Blaylock ineffective inside, but by the time he was able to run well outside, it was time to pass. And despite throwing for 381 yards, Trent Green's night wasn't as impressive as that sounds. He threw a key interception to Rodney Harrison in the end zone before the end of the first half on a ball intended for Tony Gonzalez, which greatly contributed to Kansas City's loss.

Chiefs receivers dropped two passes that could have been scores, one in the first half by Eddie Kennison and another by Johnnie Morton in the second half, while the Patriots received a huge boost with the return of Deion Branch, who caught six passes for 105 yards and a touchdown.

Daniel Graham also came up huge with three catches for 83 yards, including a 48-yarder that set the stage for Adam Vinatieri's 37-yard field goal in the second quarter.

Chiefs fans were seeing red because they knew an opportunity to turn their season around had gone by the boards.

Green managed to make a game of it by connecting on a 26-yard touchdown pass to Kennison with 6:13 remaining (though the 2-point conversion failed). The Chiefs marched 97 yards in 11 plays after the defense forced a Corey Dillon fumble at the Kansas City 3. But the Patriots got the ball back and ate up the clock behind Dillon, who fell 2 yards short of 100 and just as many short of 1,000 yards for the season. The Chiefs' D couldn't make a play to prevent Vinatieri's field goal with 1:46 left to play, which gave the Pats an 8-point lead.

"I'm disgusted," said Dillon of his fumble. "I was just trying too hard to make things happen. Immediately after that the team told me, 'We need you to come through, run the ball hard, and get us down there.' That's what I did." ⌀

Willie McGinest hauls down Kansas City QB Trent Green.

Tedy Bruschi makes an emphatic point after the Patriots downed a punt at the Ravens' 3-yard line.

Ravens

The defense dominates

24-3

BAL	0	3	0	0
NE	0	3	6	15

FOXBOROUGH
By the end of the 24-3 Patriots win over the Baltimore Ravens in Game 11, the Patriots didn't know whether to sack Kyle Boller or to hug him.

If ever the mercy rule should have applied in the last 10 minutes of a professional football game, this was the time. Boller, the second-year quarterback from Cal, was stripped of the ball, and of his dignity, in the fourth quarter when the Patriots'

Jarvis Green fell on a loose ball knocked away from Boller by Tedy Bruschi for the final score of the game.

Boller's jersey and body were covered with mud, blood, and slop in one of the more intense muggings the Patriots have handed a quarterback this season, though the four sacks the defense got credit for didn't do the beating justice.

Boller went 15 for 35 for 93

yards, with one interception and a 38.4 rating.

"He'd had a pretty good run and had been very effective," said Patriots linebacker Rosevelt Colvin of Boller. "We managed to keep control of him. If you can stop the run, then it makes any team one-dimensional, and that's what we were hoping for."

Boller said, "You want to take the dinks and dunks, but at some point you have to go deep in a game like that, and they just did a great job of protecting that."

While at halftime it was 3-3 and a defensive struggle, by the fourth quarter it was raining points — for the Patriots. New England tacked on 21 unanswered points in the second half.

Adam Vinatieri made three field goals during a rainy, windy day at Gillette Stadium, where the Patriots won their 17th straight. New England improved to 10-1 this season.

Heading into December, the only winning team on the schedule is the New York Jets, which bodes well for what might be the best regular season in Patriots history.

There were no surprises in this one.

The Ravens defense didn't allow the Patriots a touchdown until three seconds into the fourth quarter, but the Patriots were able to control the ball on the ground with Corey Dillon surpassing the 1,000-yard mark with 123 yards on 30 carries.

It was only the third time a team had surpassed 100 yards rushing against the Ravens this season, and it was just the second time Dillon had run for 100 yards or more against Ray Lewis in 11 meetings against the All-Pro middle linebacker.

Though Boller hung in there for parts of three quarters, he eventually succumbed on the Bruschi strip.

"Vrabes had him," said Bruschi, referring to linebacker Mike Vrabel. "He managed to slip away, and I was able to sack him and strip the ball from him. Then it was a case of following the ball and trying to get in there, and Jarvis was able to fall on it in the end zone."

Browns
Rout continues best start ever

NE	14	7	21	0
CLE	0	7	0	8

CLEVELAND
Their membership in the NFL elite entitles the Patriots to a gimme from time to time, like the 42-15 shellacking of the hapless Cleveland Browns.

The Patriots piled up 225 yards rushing (100 from Corey Dillon), 201 yards receiving (74 from David Patten), got a special teams touchdown before the game was 15 seconds old, and were facing a rookie quarterback on a team whose coach and executive vice president resigned during the week.

The Pats are now 11-1, continuing the best start in franchise history, and have won 26 of their last 27 games.

The speedy Bethel Johnson took heed of coach Bill Belichick's message during the week when the coach impressed on the young returner the need to grab momentum early. Evidently, Johnson was all ears, and then he was all legs.

Johnson found an opening near the 20-yard line on the opening kickoff, made a nice cut to the right, and busted loose 93 yards all the way to paydirt, shutting up the Dawg Pound.

"I don't know about quieting them, but the thing I was trying to do was worry about the emotion on our side," Johnson said. "We were coming into a hostile environment in an AFC game. I'd been close to breaking one a few times, and I know it's frustrating not to be able to do it, but we got good blocking up front, I found a seam and ran it."

The Browns are so porous that by the time Adam Vinatieri nailed the 42d point following a 44-yard Tom Brady-to-Patten touchdown, it marked the 100th point the Browns had given up in two weeks.

"All I know is that I'm having a lot of fun right now," said Troy Brown, who shadowed slot receiver Dennis Northcutt and came up with his second interception of the season — and career — in the fourth quarter. "I think the thing we always keep in mind as a team is that it doesn't matter what the score is, or what the team's record is we're playing, if you let your guard down, you're going to get beat. You have to play all-out all of the time.

"It's all mental toughness," Brown added. "It's hard to keep that up for an entire season and the teams that can do that are the teams who have a chance to win it all at the end."

Dillon earned his total on 18 carries and scored two touchdowns, but he left the game with a leg injury in the second quarter. Knowing he was 2 yards shy of 100, he campaigned to get back in and got his wish with a 2-yard carry to reach the century mark.

The Patriots ran the ball a season-high 50 times, also utilizing Kevin Faulk, who gained 87 yards on 13 carries, and rookie Cedric Cobbs, who ran for 29 yards on 16 carries.

Bengals

The defense picks its spots

35-28

CIN	0	14	7	7
NE	7	21	7	0

FOXBOROUGH

When a team is 12-1, clinching a playoff berth and the AFC East title in spite of allowing almost 500 yards of offense, what else can one do but project this type of performance down the road to more meaningful games?

What if the Patriots' defense allows almost 500 yards to the Indianapolis Colts, or to Pittsburgh, in January? What if they play a team whose quarterback doesn't throw an interception for a touchdown, as Carson Palmer did in a 35-28 Patriots win over Cincinnati at Gillette Stadium?

"The offense definitely bailed out the defense," Patriots defensive lineman Richard Seymour said after the win.

On the day offensive coordinator Charlie Weis accepted the Notre Dame head coaching job, New England's offense put up 28 points and certainly made Weis look good (an offense minus Notre Dame's own David Givens, who sustained a leg injury Saturday).

Yet the defense did three very important things. Asante Samuel intercepted a Palmer pass and ran it back 34 yards for a touchdown. Rodney Harrison hit Rudi Johnson and caused him to fumble on Cincinnati's opening drive at the Patriots' 12. And Troy Brown intercepted a Jon Kitna end-zone pass in the fourth quarter.

"We just can't let a team go up and down the field like that," Harrison said.

"We just weren't able to stop them. We're happy to get the win, don't get me wrong. But we can and have to play a lot better than this. That was a very explosive team we faced. It's not anything we didn't anticipate, but we have to do a better job stopping them."

Nor was it a great day for the Patriots' special teams, which allowed a fake field goal for a score by punter Kyle Larson, who took the snap and rambled 11 yards for the Bengals' third score with 3:10 left in the third quarter.

But, as in most games when the Patriots aren't artistically strong, they wait for the other team to shoot itself in the foot. The Bengals had a very good chance to score on their opening possession. Palmer, who left the game late in the third quarter with a knee sprain, engineered an impressive drive before Johnson coughed up the ball on a good smack from Harrison, allowing Willie McGinest to recover.

The tone was set right there.

"You've got to get points there," Palmer said. "Obviously points would have been big. We had two turnovers in the red zone and you just can't do that against the Super Bowl champions. We left points out there, and that makes all the difference in a game like this."

Tom Brady, who came out of a mini slump in his previous two games to complete 18 of 26 passes for 260 yards and two touchdowns (48 yards to David Patten and 17 to Christian Fauria) for a 127.1 quarterback rating, made the Bengals hurt a little bit more.

He directed a 13-play, 84-yard drive, making five first downs, three in a row to begin the drive. They came on pass plays of 23 yards to Deion Branch and 16 yards to Patten, and in between Corey Dillon, facing his old teammates for the first time in the regular season, rumbled for 16 yards. Dillon carried 22 times on the day, gaining 88 yards. ⬭

Dolphins

Squished by a lowly nemesis

28-29

NE	7	7	7	7
MIA	7	3	7	12

MIAMI

Hell was freezing over. Pigs were flying. And the Dolphins were beating the Patriots.

When A.J. Feeley found 6-foot-2-inch receiver Derrius Thompson for a 21-yard scoring pass over 5-10 Troy Brown with 1:23 remaining in the game on a fourth and 10, it capped an amazing night for the lowly Miami Dolphins, who staged their Super Bowl at Pro Player Stadium in a 29-28 victory, handing the Patriots their second loss of the season.

The winning score was set up by Tom Brady's third of four interceptions, to linebacker Brendon Ayanbadejo after Jason Taylor had Brady in his grasp on third down inside the Patriots 20. Brady was trying to get the ball to Daniel Graham, in what surely would have clinched it for the Patriots.

Brady still had 1:17 to lead a comeback, but he was sacked by David Bowens for a 9-yard loss and then free safety Arturo Freeman finished it off with the fourth INT on a pass intended for David Givens at the Patriot 37.

"They got cocky today," Freeman said. "They felt they were the defending champions and could make plays all over the field. We are the only team, if you check history, that New England has a problem playing against."

For the first time since Halloween,

Christian Fauria takes to the air after catching a 17-yard TD pass.

Tom Brady is headed for a fall, as are the Patriots, after this ill-advised pass was intercepted.

when they bowed to the Steelers, the Patriots experienced the opposing quarterback taking a knee to end the game. And for the first time this year the Patriots were second fiddle to the Steelers, who are 13-1 to the Patriots' 12-2. The Dolphins improved to 3-11.

Brown blamed himself for the Thompson catch, saying, "I didn't make the play. I've got to do everything I can to keep him from catching that."

The New England locker room was understandably quiet after the game. Brady, who was sacked twice and knocked down numerous times, said, "I found out a long time ago you're not going to win too many games throwing four interceptions."

Of the interception to Ayanbadejo, Brady said, "It was just a bad play. I thought I could get it to Dan. I thought I had time to throw, but my arm got ripped and I just pulled it right to the guy. It's just not a good play, and if we want to win games we can't do that. We've got to play better and it starts with me."

Brady's poor night overshadowed a good game by Corey Dillon, who carried 26 times for 121 yards. Dillon helped eat up 4:57 on a 65-yard drive that gave the Patriots a 28-17 lead with 3:59 left to play.

But the Dolphins were able to respond in 1:52, going 68 yards on seven plays. The drive was capped by Sammy Morris's 1-yard plunge after Patriots safety Rodney Harrison had been flagged for interference in the end zone against Chris Chambers. The Dolphins failed to execute the 2-point conversion, and there was 2:07 left on the clock.

The Patriots were unable to run that out and the Dolphins were not to be denied.

"We had an 11-point lead and we blew it," said Harrison. "They made plays in the end and we made mistakes. We were prepared to play, we just didn't execute. It's not the end of the world. We're obviously disappointed."

Jets
Intentional grounding
23 – 7

NE	0	13	3	7
NYJ	0	0	0	7

EAST RUTHERFORD
The message Willie McGinest and the other Patriots received from the coaches was simple — win the game and earn a bye week. It wasn't exactly something they needed to be hit over the head with, but they knew it was there for the taking.

"All week long the coaches told us, 'This is what you've played all season for,' and they were right," said McGinest. "We prepared well all week. We put last week behind us and we went out and did what we're capable of as a team. We put together three phases of the game and we beat a good team, a divisional rival, on their turf."

After completing the 23-7 shellacking of the Jets, coach Bill Belichick decided that talk of bye weeks was the old message, and any discussion of the topic should be eliminated from the players' conversation.

The goal for the last week of the season was a chance to match last year's 14-2 mark by beating the San Francisco 49ers at Gillette Stadium.

"It's significant because we haven't had a week off since early in the season," said wide receiver/defensive back Troy Brown. "It's always important to achieve these goals along the way. We

Eugene Wilson savors his fourth-quarter interception, which set up a Deion Branch TD.

got one today. We responded to what we needed to do."

And the Jets sure didn't.

The Jets have been hearing questions all season by members of the New York media about their problem beating elite teams. The questioning usually gets a surly reaction from the players.

A couple of weeks back, when asked about beating "soft" teams, New York center Kevin Mawae said, "San Diego is 9-3. We beat them on the road. San Diego is not a good team right now? Are they a good team right now? They are a playoff contender. We beat a playoff contender on the road. We're 9-3. Put that in your [notebook]. Ridiculous."

Then Chad Pennington chastised the media last week because they kept writing that he can't beat a good team. The Patriots' dominance yesterday, meaning the Jets missed a chance to clinch a wild-card berth, didn't make Pennington's and Mawae's cases look very strong.

Along with an effective job by the Patriots' front seven, Tom Brady rebounded marvelously from a four-interception performance against the Dolphins in Miami, taking the 77,975 fans at the Meadowlands out of the game early on a frigid day.

Brady tossed two touchdowns and threw for 264 yards with no interceptions in an impressive road performance.

The only hostility from the fans was directed at their own players (the Jets were booed off the field at halftime) and the play-calling of offensive coordinator Paul Hackett.

"[The Patriots] just came down here, and as I told our football team, they flat-out kicked our behinds — on offense, defense, and special teams," said Jets coach Herm Edwards. "That is how it all boils down. We knew what was at stake. We needed to win a game at home to get back into the playoffs and we didn't do it." ✐

49ers
It all adds up to a fitting finish

SF	7	0	0	0
NE	0	7	7	7

FOXBOROUGH

The coach perhaps has gotten the biggest piece of the credit pie for the Patriots' success the last four seasons, but yesterday Bill Belichick gladly cut the largest piece for his players for enduring a season of injuries and the pressures associated with staying atop the mountain during a second consecutive 14-win season.

"For what they've been through this year, I think you have to give a lot of credit to the players for their diligence, their perseverance, and for battling all the way through," Belichick said following a 21-7 victory over the 49ers in the season finale at Gillette Stadium. "It has been a long season and they played well enough today and we're happy with that. It's on to the playoffs."

"I don't know who we play next," Belichick said. "It doesn't make any difference. Whoever it is will be pretty good and we know that. I'm glad we ended up on top and ended up with a 14-2 record. I thought the players deserved that for what they have done this year."

There was a sense all week the players wanted to end on a high note, match last season's 14-win total, and go undefeated at home in back-to-back seasons.

A captains' meeting with Belichick late in the week bore that out; the captains spoke of needing some momentum heading into the playoffs.

Besides the win, the other major highlights were escaping the game with all of their major players healthy, and Corey Dillon eclipsing the 1,600-yard mark to earn a $375,000 incentive.

"This is good for us," said left tackle Matt Light. "We haven't been able to take the foot off the pedal all season. This week will be a well-deserved break for us."

Most of the starters came out at some point late in the game, although they probably had to play longer than expected because it took them a while to get going. The Patriots trailed, 7-0, for the first time in the last 24 games.

It wasn't until the start of the fourth quarter, with New England driving for its third score, that Rohan Davey relieved Tom Brady. Brady threw 30 passes, completing 22 for 226 yards and two touchdowns.

Dillon left after eclipsing the 1,600-yard mark when he went off right guard for 29 yards to the 14 with 10:19 left in the third quarter. With 116 yards, he went over the 100-yard mark for the ninth time this season, and helped the Patriots run for a 4.07-yards-per-carry average, the best since the 1985 team.

The Patriots ran it 524 times for 2,134 yards this season, throwing it 485 times for 3,750 gross yards.

Dillon returned at the start of the fourth quarter, coinciding with the appearance of Davey, and scored his 12th rushing touchdown.

"[Running backs coach] Ivan [Fears] told me to go back in," Dillon said. "I don't know what the big deal is. I don't find it weird at all."

Dillon escaped his 14-carry workload with no injuries. He seemed relatively happy after the game, as did all the Patriots, who finally can exhale for a week. ✐

Deion Branch and Tom Brady make connections after combining for an 8-yard touchdown play.

BY JOHN POWERS

IMAGE IS EVERYTHING

TEAM TAKES ITS 'TYPE OF GUY' AND WINS, THE PATRIOT WAY

Socrates, who lived back around the time of Papa Bear Halas, had the championship formula figured out a couple of millennia before Super Bowl I. "Know thyself," the Greek philosopher preached.

Pro football teams and their followers may talk about philosophies, systems and programs, but success and failure essentially are questions of self-knowledge. In the NFL, identity usually determines destiny.

"Knowing who you are and what you want to be," muses ABC Sports analyst John Madden. "What is an Oakland Raider? What is a Seattle Seahawk? What is a Dallas Cowboy? If you can't answer that, therein lies the problem. What is an Arizona Cardinal? I have no idea."

By now, after winning two Super Bowls in three seasons, the Patriots have an identity that is recognized far beyond Foxborough. "Intelligent, efficient, businesslike, physical, adaptable, flexible," says Giants general manager Ernie Accorsi. "Play well in the clutch, win tough road games..."

The storied professional football franchises, such as Green Bay, Pittsburgh, Miami, Dallas, San Francisco, never had a problem with mistaken identity. The Packers were about discipline and professionalism, the 49ers about flair and imagination, the Cowboys about innovation and precision, the Dolphins about poise and resourcefulness, the Steelers about smashmouth straightforwardness.

Even the new franchises, whose trophy cases still are bare, have identities-in-progress. "Our identity is, we play hard," says Houston Texans general manager Charley Casserly. "If you come to play us, it's a 60-minute football game."

The Patriots are about focus, pragmatism, diligence, versatility, resilience, selflessness. "They aren't a team of superstars," says Pittsburgh president Art Rooney II, whose team handed the Patriots the first of their two defeats this season and has now twice lost to them for the right to go to

the Super Bowl. "They're not looking for the other guy to make the play."

For most of their 45 years, the Patriots had a negative identity. They were the Patsies, fortune's fools, playing beneath a persistent rain cloud. Silly things happened to them, most of their own making. "They were No. 4 in that town forever," says Casserly of Boston's four major pro teams. He spent a decade in Springfield as a student, coach, and administrator. "And it wasn't close between 4 and 3."

The slapstick image began changing in 1993 when Bill Parcells was hired, and the Patriots went from 2-14 to the Super Bowl in four seasons. "They hired a proven winner who had won two Super Bowls," says Casserly, who was with the Redskins when they won three titles. "That gave them a new identity immediately."

The Patsies persona vanished three years ago when New England upset the St. Louis Rams for its first championship. The new persona, built around preparation and passion, was reinforced last February when the Patriots defeated the Carolina Panthers for their second crown.

CAN'T ARGUE WITH SUCCESS

"The way Bill Belichick is doing it right now is the best way," says Kansas City Chiefs coach Dick Vermeil, who made it to the Super Bowl with both the Eagles and Rams. "They're winning the most football games, so that makes it the best way."

With their AFC title victory over Pittsburgh, the Patriots have won 31 of their last 33 games. That stretch included a league-record 21 straight wins, which Belichick saw as 21 one-game winning streaks. His team's record, he says, is now 0-0, just as it was last year at this time. That approach — an obsession with what's dead ahead — is what makes the Patriots who they are now. What-ifs don't concern them.

"It's a core part of our philosophy," says Patriots vice president Scott Pioli, who's in charge of player personnel.

"Hypotheticals don't matter. It's wasted time, wasted energy, rather than what's real and what's right in front of you."

The Belichick credo is practical, absolute: "Whatever it is, it is." If Drew Bledsoe goes down, if the linebackers and cornerbacks start dropping, you plug in different people and you deal with it.

"You just try to take the situation at hand and do the best you can with it," says Belichick. "When it is over, recalibrate, reload, and go again. That is where we have been all season. We never sat there and thought, 'Well, if this happens, where are we going to be two months from now?' We just never look at it like that."

The schedule says you play on Sunday and the rules say you must have 11 men on the field. Sometimes, that means using a receiver as a cornerback. But you show up and you perform, however you must.

"You just think about, 'Here's who we're playing this week. What are we going to do? What is our best chance to do it?' " says Belichick. "You jump off the ship and you start swimming. You don't really worry about where you are going. You are just trying to make good time."

It's not as if the Patriots plunge overboard without a life preserver, a compass, and shark repellent. What sets them apart from most of their rivals is that they're meticulously prepared and that everyone — from owner Bob Kraft to Belichick to the assistant coaches to the scouts to the players to the trainers to the equipment people — is on the same page.

"They have the strongest philosophy in those terms," says Madden, who coached the eye-patched Raiders (has any team had a clearer identity?) to their first Super Bowl victory. "This is the way you play football as a New England Patriot. This is how you play on offense. This is how you play on defense. This is how you play on special teams. They have a system for everything and they teach it better than anybody."

There is a Patriot Way now, just as there has been a Packer Way, a Dolphin

Way, a Cowboy Way, a 49er Way, a Steeler Way. All of them revolve around what former San Francisco coach Bill Walsh calls "a central belief system."

Some, like Pittsburgh's, which is based on robust running and uncivil defense, go back decades. "Even when we didn't have very good teams, people would say that even if the Steelers didn't beat you, you felt like you'd gotten beat up after you played them," says Rooney.

CONSISTENT MESSAGE

Much of the Steeler identity comes from having had one owner (the Rooney family) for their 71 years and only two coaches (Chuck Noll and Bill Cowher) since 1969. When Kraft bought the Patriots in 1994, they had had three owners, four coaches, and four quarterbacks in seven years. "Stability and continuity are critical," says Pioli.

Now they've had the same owner for 11 years, the same head coach for five, the same quarterback for four. But equally significant is the stability and continuity of expectations. There's no confusion, no dissension, about how to reach their goals. "We do what we say we're going to do," says Pioli.

The clarity and simplicity of purpose comes from Belichick, who has been around long enough now to shape his team in his image.

"For better or worse, it's impossible for a football team not to take on the personality of its head coach," Accorsi says. "You can see that the Steelers are Cowher and that the Patriots are Bill."

Pro football isn't primarily about philosophies and systems, about schemes and tendencies, playbooks and scouting reports.

"It all starts with people," says Vermeil. "You have to have a foundation of things you believe in. You have concepts and philosophies that you operate by. But I always start with people. Then, I worry about how we're going to do things."

The challenge, for the Patriots and

everybody else in the league, is finding what teams call "our kind of guy."

"Everyone wants big, fast, tough, smart guys who love the game," says Jacksonville executive scout Terry McDonough, who worked with Belichick and Pioli in Cleveland.

The Patriots clearly know what they don't want. "A player who has limited ability and a player who is a bad character guy," says defensive coordinator Romeo Crennel. "If you fit that criteria, you don't fit in."

What the Patriots are looking for are players with football character.

"We're concerned about what the players are like as people and what things are important to them," says Pioli. "What their overall makeup is, what motivates them, how much pride they have. Essentially, how important football is to them. There's no test that will tell you that. It's a combination of observing, of asking questions, of gathering information."

The core question is: Can he be a Patriot? "We're not for everyone, and not everyone is for us," says Pioli.

The three Patriotic essentials are commitment, focus, and discipline.

"Being where you're supposed to be when you're supposed to be there and doing your job," says Pioli. "That's what discipline is."

By that standard, Tom Brady is the team's star-spangled poster boy. Even during the bye week, he was thinking "all day, every day" about all three of New England's potential playoff opponents.

"What is the price you would pay for success?" he muses. "What would you give up to win this game?"

'OUR TYPE OF GUYS'

Brady was the 199th player chosen in the 2000 draft. Who would have predicted that he would quarterback the team to two Super Bowls?

"I don't think we would have been talking about Brady like that before the 2001 season," says Belichick. "Who is this guy?

Some guy from Michigan? A sixth-round pick? What's the big deal about him?"

The big deal was Brady's intangibles (a word the Patriot brass dismiss; every quality is tangible, they insist). No quarterback in the league manages a game better. But that wasn't obvious until Drew Bledsoe got hurt and Brady stepped in.

"It's a very unscientific business at times," concedes Belichick. "That's why there are so many mistakes in the draft, in personnel and free agency. Put guys in different systems, put them in different opportunities, it turns out differently."

You don't have to be a top draft pick to start for the Patriots. Wide receiver David Givens was a seventh-round pick, center Dan Koppen a fifth. But the Patriots had a sense they would blossom in Foxborough.

"Bill and Scott start with bringing in our type of guys," says offensive coordinator Charlie Weis. "Then our job as coaches is to fit them in. Don't say, 'Well, he can't do this.' Find out what he can do. We never look at a player as somebody we can't use."

The Belichick philosophy is that football players play football. Why can't Mike Vrabel catch touchdown passes? Why can't kicker Adam Vinatieri throw them? Why can't tight end Christian Fauria defend on Hail Mary plays? Why can't receiver Troy Brown fill in at cornerback?

The Patriots' remarkable ability to be whatever they have to be on a given Sunday has made them difficult to label. They aren't "The Greatest Show on Turf," they have no "Steel Curtain" or "Doomsday Defense." They just know how to put one W after another. That's the Patriot Way.

Parcells, who has logged 16 seasons as a head coach with four NFL teams, has a theory about football identities. "You are what you are," he likes to say.

If you're 2-14, you're 2-14. And if you're 14-2...

The Patsies who used to live at this address were somebody else. These Pats have rings on two fingers and are going for a third. They are what they are. ✍

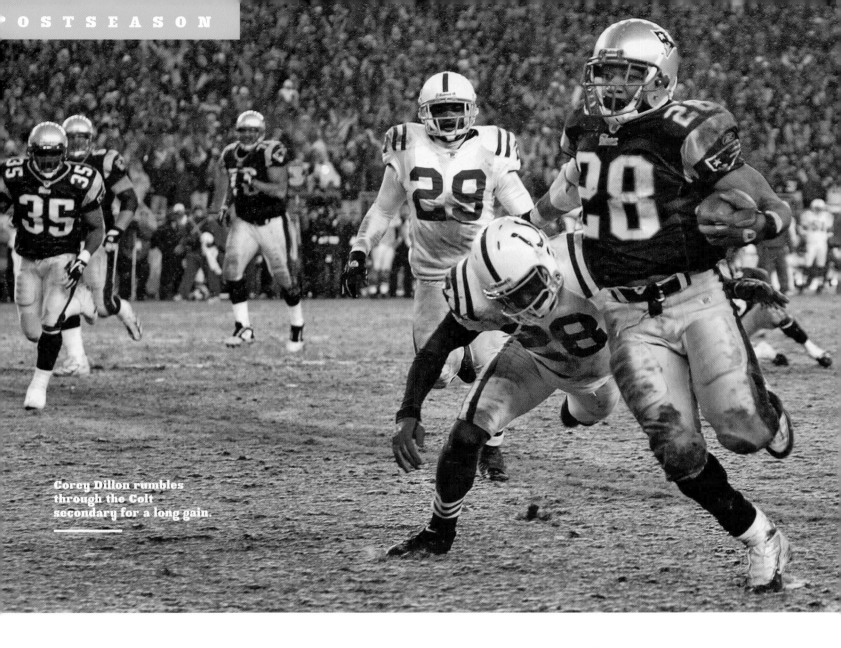

Corey Dillon rumbles through the Colt secondary for a long gain.

Doubters out in force

The majority of national writers and analysts, and some local scribes, are leaning toward the Colts to end whatever magic the Patriots have been able to spin over Peyton Manning. What gives?

AFC DIVISIONAL PLAYOFF / COLTS SAFETY RODNEY HARRISON HAS A TEAM-HIGH 11 TACKLES AND MAKES THE GAME'S ONLY

Rodney Harrison makes the tackle and Tedy Bruschi makes the smooth pickup.

Colts

Again, Manning stopped Colt

20-3

IND	0	3	0	0
NE	0	6	7	7

FOXBOROUGH

All week the message was clear. "You have to slow him down," said the experts. "You have to get him out of his rhythm." The Patriots went one better — they stopped Peyton Manning cold.

Maybe the signs and the chants were a little harsh during the Patriots' 20-3 pounding of the Colts and Manning, which punched New England's ticket to the AFC Championship Game in Pittsburgh.

"After the game you will get your ring — suffer-ring," read one. The crowd was yelling, "Cut that meat! Cut that meat!" in reference to Manning's ad campaign in which he cheers for the common folk while they're performing their jobs.

The NFL MVP was just that yesterday — common. Manning (27 of 42, 238 yards, one interception) was unable to lead his vaunted offense to the end zone, and his longest completion was 18 yards.

The Patriots, who were without Pro Bowl defenders Ty Law and Richard Seymour, played it the way some experts thought they would — jamming receivers at the line, rushing three, occasionally sending a blitzing linebacker to knock Manning off his rhythm, and covering well. They never allowed the Colt receivers to get free downfield.

They disguised their defense by sometimes dropping eight men into coverage and sometimes going with as few as four defensive backs.

The Colts coaching staff had no answers. It also had no answers for the steady snow that fell throughout the game, accompanied by a swirling wind.

The Patriots also adopted another much talked-about suggestion — they controlled the clock for 37:43 with three massive scoring drives of 16, 15, and 14 plays which ate up a total of 24:47. Two of the lengthy drives came in the second half when the Patriots completely took over.

Corey Dillon carried 23 times for 144 yards, while Tom Brady played a mistake-free game, completing 18 of 27 passes for 144 yards, one score, and no interceptions.

The Patriots seemed buoyed by Mike Vanderjagt's "ripe for the picking" comment earlier in the week.

They were buoyed by the media members who dismissed their chances of stopping the Colts.

"I guess the panel of experts were wrong, huh?" said Matt Light, who shrugged off an early illegal motion penalty on a fourth and goal at the 1-yard line, which nullified a Corey Dillon touchdown and ultimately cost the Patriots 4 points after they settled for Adam Vinatieri's 24-yard field goal.

The Patriots converted 53 percent (8 for 15) on third down, including 6 of 8 in the second half. As has been their trademark, they made big plays at big times.

None was bigger than Tedy Bruschi's strip of Dominic Rhodes at the Patriots 39-yard line with 3:18 remaining in the second quarter. Bruschi wrestled the ball away after Rhodes caught a Manning pass for a 2-yard loss.

The Patriots easily could have gone into the half trailing, 7-6, but the defense forced the Colts to settle for Vanderjagt's 23-yard field goal as time expired. It was the one time Manning had been able to sustain a long drive. Manning connected on passes of 13, 16, 11, and 10 yards during the 11-play, 67-yard drive, which nearly ended on an interception, but the ball slipped through Eugene Wilson's hands in the end zone.

"We would have liked to have gotten a touchdown there," Colts coach Tony Dungy said. Holding the Colts to a field goal over the first 30 minutes was amazing enough. The Patriots did it with Asante Samuel blanketing Marvin Harrison, Randall Gay shadowing Reggie Wayne, and Brown covering Brandon Stokley.

The linebackers took turns on tight end Dallas Clark. Elder statesman Roman Phifer, not known for his coverage skills, did an admirable job.

"We heard all week we couldn't cover all of their guys, but I think we did a good job," said Samuel, who did a solid job filling in for Law, holding Harrison to five catches and 44 yards. Both teams had futile series to open the second half, but the Patriots settled in and played what Bill Belichick called "our best 30 minutes of football." Beginning a drive at their 13, the Patriots steadily used Dillon and Kevin Faulk to move down the field. They got a big 14-yard pass play from Brady to Patrick Pass on a third-and-3, which advanced it to the Indianapolis 24. And then it was Faulk and Dillon to the 5, where Brady hit David Givens for the first touchdown of the game.

"Everyone doubted us," said Patriots defensive end Jarvis Green, who filled in so admirably for Seymour. "They said we couldn't do it. It was very emotional for us. The last two years have been great. We won 28 games and lost only four." 🏈

MVP Peyton Manning can see that he is about to fall to 0-7 against Bill Belichick's Patriots.

Steelers

It's curtains for Pittsburgh

41 - 27

NE	10	14	7	10
PIT	3	0	14	10

PITTSBURGH

Seven minutes and seven seconds remained in the first quarter when it became evident that the Patriots were going to win the AFC title at Heinz Field.

The Steelers had decided to go for it on fourth and 1 at the Patriots' 39-yard line. It wasn't the biggest or the most important play because it came so early, but it seemed to crystalize what the Patriots, who were about to win their third AFC Championship in four years, were all about.

Before the Steelers came up to the line of scrimmage, coach Bill Belichick summoned middle linebacker Ted Johnson and offered some advice. Johnson, who calls the defensive signals, took that advice back to the huddle. Moments later, Jerome Bettis took a handoff from Ben Roethlisberger and was stopped dead in his tracks by Rosevelt Colvin, who stripped the ball loose. Mike Vrabel made the recovery.

"[Belichick] saw something and he alerted me and it turned out to be huge. It was an adjustment — I really can't go into it," said Johnson. "That stuff happens all the time. It's amazing sometimes."

So many small things added up to a 41-27 win over the Steelers, sending New England to Super Bowl XXXIX in

Deion Branch hauls in a 60-yard TD catch (left) on the way to 153 total yards.

COMMIT JUST ONE 5-YARD PENALTY AND NO TURNOVERS; VINATIERI'S 48-YARD FIELD GOAL MATCHES THE LONGEST

IN FOUR-YEAR-OLD HEINZ FIELD HISTORY; RODNEY HARRISON AND TEDY BRUSCHI TIE FOR THE TEAM LEAD WITH SEVEN

Patriots lineman
Matt Light
signals the final
touchdown.

Jacksonville. If the Patriots have a
to-do list, you can be sure every item
has been checked off.

New England stopped the Steelers'
inside running game, holding Bettis to
64 yards on 17 carries. They rattled
Roethlisberger, who had three interceptions, including one that was
returned 87 yards for a touchdown by
Rodney Harrison, boosting the
visitors' lead to 24-3 late in the first
half. The Pats solved Pittsburgh's
vaunted zone blitz as Tom Brady, who
improved to 8-0 in the postseason, had
another of his money games, completing 14 of 21 attempts for 207 yards, a
pair of touchdowns, no interceptions,
and a 130.5 passer rating.

In addition to Harrison and Brady,
Deion Branch and Corey Dillon also
came up with big plays.

Branch caught four passes for 116
yards and a touchdown and rushed
twice for 37 yards and another score.

Dillon rushed 24 times for 73 yards,
including a huge 25-yard scoring run in
the third. Let's not forget a pair of interceptions by Eugene Wilson and a
Heinz Field record-tying 48-yard field
goal by Adam Vinatieri.

It was as if the Patriots sent a gift to
millions of New Englanders trapped in
their homes as a result of the weekend
blizzard.

"This is for all the fans," said
Patriots owner Bob Kraft, who accepted the Lamar Hunt Trophy after the
game from AFC representative Joe
Namath. "We have the greatest fans in
the country and we know that the
weather is tough up there and we wanted this for them."

The Patriots created their own blizzard on the field. They had been
smacked around in a 34-20 loss here on
Halloween.

All week they had watched film of
how badly they had played. The
Patriots were embarrassed and you can

TACKLES EACH; DEION BRANCH HAS FOUR RECEPTIONS, AVERAGING 29 YARDS PER CATCH; THE PATRIOTS ARE 14-0

be sure that Belichick reminded them plenty.

"We played Patriots football," nose tackle Keith Traylor said. "We were physical from the opening play. We came out with an attitude and they fought back. Coach [Bill] Cowher's teams never quit and they didn't."

The Patriots' 21-game winning streak ended here Oct. 31, but last night the Patriots ended Pittsburgh's 15-game win streak in what was a far more devastating loss.

Traylor was right about the Steelers not quitting. Pittsburgh scored two touchdowns and a field goal to pull within 11 points with 13:29 remaining.

thought there was too much time to go with 2 yards to come away with nothing. That was my decision and I would do it again," Cowher said.

The Patriots had received a big break on another play involving Givens, who had caught an 18-yard pass and appeared to fumble. Officials ruled cornerback Willie Williams had recovered, but a look by the replay judge revealed that Givens's knee had hit the ground. A 15-yard unnecessary roughness penalty on Clark Haggans was tacked on.

On the next play, Dillon, who had been contained quite nicely by the Steelers, ran around the right side

end zone.

"That was at least a 10-point swing, maybe more," Belichick said.

The Patriots had gone ahead, 17-3, on a five-play drive in which Brady connected on a 46-yard pass and great catch by Branch, who caught the ball while getting hit by Troy Polamalu at the Steelers' 14.

Two plays later, Brady appeared to check off at the line when he spotted the defense playing off Givens. Brady hit Givens with a quick toss, freezing Williams, who slipped and allowed Givens to run 9 yards untouched into the end zone.

The Patriots forced two early turnovers, the first when Wilson picked off

These Patriot playoff wins are like Ray Charles songs, Nantucket sunsets, and hot fudge sundaes. Each one is better than the last.

Both teams were aided by overturned plays on challenges which led to scores.

The Steelers got their break when David Givens made what appeared to be a 44-yard catch over the middle for a first down at the Steelers' 28. But before Brady could run the next play, Cowher tossed the red beanbag and officials overturned the call, ruling the ball hit the ground. That forced the Patriots to punt.

The Steelers started at their 45 following a 22-yard return by Antwaan Randle El and drove to the New England 2. But on fourth and goal, Cowher sent in Jeff Reed, who drilled a 20-yard field goal.

"I think with 13½ minutes to go, to only be down by 11 points, which is just two scores — a field goal, a touchdown, and a 2-point conversion — I

behind Stephen Neal for a 25-yard TD to give the Pats a 31-10 lead.

The Steelers had scored on their first possession of the third quarter when Roethlisberger, whose right hand had been soothed with cold water late in the first half, came out with an air of confidence. He led the Steelers on a five-play, 56-yard drive, the big play a 34-yard pass to Randle El. Bettis took it in from the 5.

Harrison's 87-yard interception return for a touchdown, which made it 24-3 with 2:14 remaining in the first half, broke the Steelers' back.

Roethlisberger stepped back and tried to throw it to the right side to tight end Jerame Tuman. Harrison jumped the route, snagged the pass, and was helped by a Mike Vrabel block on Roethlisberger as he jogged, then walked, into the

Roethlisberger's first pass. The rookie overthrew Randle El for his eighth interception in his last 87 throws.

The first of two Branch reverses — the second one resulted in a 23-yard touchdown run in the fourth — seemed to loosen the Steeler defense. That led to Vinatieri's long field goal.

It was after the big fourth-and-1 stop of Bettis in the first quarter that Patriots offensive coordinator Charlie Weis went for the jugular.

Starting at his 40, Brady hit Branch in stride at about the 5-yard line and the speedy receiver stumbled in from there. Brady made the play work when he looked over the middle, which drew Polamalu over and left Branch alone with Deshea Townsend. The 60-yard touchdown reception is the longest in Patriots postseason history. ⌀

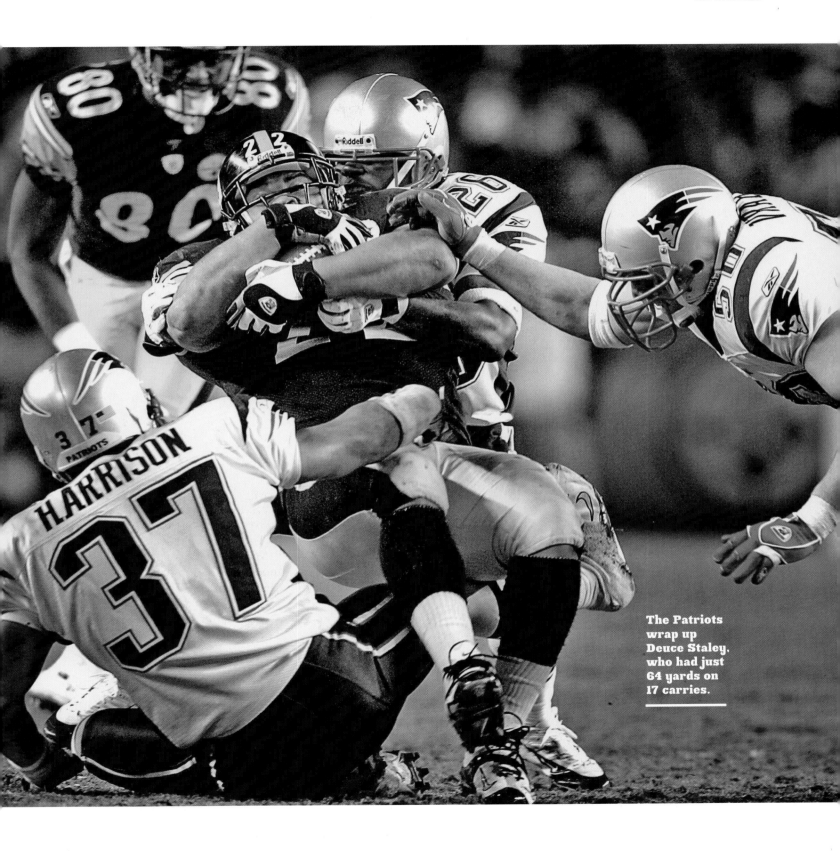

The Patriots wrap up Deuce Staley, who had just 64 yards on 17 carries.

TYING VINCE LOMBARDI; THE PATRIOTS DEFEATED THE STEELERS FOR THE SECOND TIME AT HEINZ FIELD FOR THE AFC TITLE

Dynasty

SUPER BOWL XXXIX

Eagles

Triple-crown winners

24 - 21

NE	0	7	7	10
PHI	0	7	7	7

It's done. Two straight. Three out of four. the Patriots stand astride the professional football world. With three out of four, what the Patriots have done for themselves is gain a seat at the mythical Council of Football Greats, along with the Packers, Steelers, 49ers, and Cowboys during the Super Bowl era.

SUPER BOWL XXXIX / EAGLES THE PATRIOTS ARE SEVEN-POINT FAVORITES HEADING INTO THE GAME; PUNTER JOSH

Kevin Faulk
runs away
from the
Eagles'
Jeremiah
Trotter.

JACKSONVILLE

The red, white, and blue confetti floated in the sky and dropped ever so gently on their latest field of dreams.

There were hugs, pats on the backs, and family moments with children hugging their hero dads, and wives kissing their hero husbands. There was Bill Belichick, Romeo Crennel, and Charlie Weis, the brain trust of the Super Bowl XXXIX champions embracing for the final time, with Weis off to Notre Dame and Crennel off to Cleveland.

The Vince Lombardi Trophy was touched, kissed, and embraced like a loved one. The New England Patriots, draped in blood, sweat, and tears, won the Super Bowl for the third time in four years, beating the Philadelphia Eagles, 24-21, before 78,125 at Alltel Stadium.

Dynasty?

"We're champions now," said Patriots safety Rodney Harrison. "I don't know about dynasty right now."

Football historians will look back upon the current run by the Patriots and decide if it is indeed a dynasty. But for now it's clear that no football team in the world is better.

The Patriots broke a 14-14 tie and took control with two fourth-quarter scores against the Eagles, who couldn't stop Tom Brady and company when it counted most.

Brady completed 23 of 33 passes for 236 yards and two touchdowns for a 110.2 quarterback rating. He was the calm, cool quarterback who had been there and done that. His Eagles counterpart, Donovan McNabb (30 of 51 for 357 yards, three touchdowns, and three interceptions), looked jittery at times in his Super Bowl debut.

Brady's favorite target was Deion Branch, who tied a Super Bowl record with 11 catches for 133 yards and was named the game's most valuable player.

The Patriots boosted their lead to 24-14 in the fourth quarter courtesy of Adam Vinatieri's 22-yard field goal, which capped an eight-play, 43-yard drive.

McNabb, who has a history of overthrowing receivers at crucial times, got the ball with 5:40 remaining and tried to rally the Eagles.

The Patriots played another stout defensive game, showing McNabb looks — including lining up two linemen and five linebackers — he may have never seen on film. They had to adapt after losing free safety Eugene Wilson for more than half the game with what was thought to be a broken arm.

The Eagles pulled within 24-21 with 1:48 remaining when McNabb found Greg Lewis for a 30-yard touchdown pass over rookie safety Dexter Reid — Wilson's replacement. That capped a 13-play, 79-yard drive that consumed 3 minutes 52 seconds.

The Eagles attempted an onside kick, but it was recovered by Christian Fauria at the Eagles' 41. While the Eagles forced a Patriots punt, McNabb couldn't pull off the heroics, with Harrison icing the game with his second interception.

While the Eagles received a strong performance from Terrell Owens (nine catches, 122 yards), the flamboyant receiver never found the end zone.

You could sense the Patriots were taking over late in the second quarter, and by the time Paul McCartney had finished "Hey Jude" at halftime, Belichick's troops were ready to take the field and carry on the momentum.

Offensive coordinator Weis said the 25-minute halftime allowed him time to figure out how to beat the Eagle blitz. "They were blitzing up the middle with [Jeremiah Trotter] in an attempt to make Brady get out of the pocket and so we had to do something to combat it. We used the screens and the shorter passing game and it really opened things up for us," Weis said.

Brady was picking it up very nicely, spotting Branch for gains of 27 and 21, the latter giving the Patriots a first down at the Philadelphia 2-yard line. From there, Brady went to designated short-yardage tight end Mike Vrabel, who gathered a tipped pass for his second touchdown reception in as many Super Bowls, giving the champs a 14-7 lead with 11:09 left in the third.

Yet the Eagles answered quickly, evening things at 14 with 3:35 remaining in the third. It was turning into a heavyweight title fight, and McNabb appeared poised for the challenge.

The Eagles targeted rookie corner Randall Gay, throwing at him often during the drive. McNabb completed passes of 15, 4, and 10 to Brian Westbrook, the last catch good for 6 points. He also found Lewis and Owens twice each on the drive. His favorite first-half target, Todd Pinkston, was cramping up and was in the locker room receiving intravenous fluids.

The chains kept moving and even with a blitzing Willie McGinest coming at him, McNabb managed to drill a pass to Westbrook between two Patriots for the tying score.

With the score even after three quarters (a Super Bowl first), the Patriots started a well-orchestrated drive to regain the lead. Brady was very methodical in leading the Patriots 66 yards, using Kevin Faulk as a key component.

Faulk caught passes of 13 and 14 yards (both beating Eagle blitzes) and ran twice for 20 yards in picking up three first downs on the drive. Corey Dillon capped it with a 2-yard touchdown run off left tackle with 13:44 remaining, giving the Patriots a 21-14 lead.

"We were 0 for 4 on first downs in the first quarter and we really couldn't get into any rhythm offensively," said Brady. "We just didn't move the ball. We tried to run it and didn't gain a whole lot of yards. We made a few more plays in the second half." ✐

THE EAGLES TO ONLY 45 YARDS RUSHING; NEW ENGLAND COMMITS JUST ONE TURNOVER, THE EAGLES COMMIT FOUR;

"I don't think they were looking to throw me the ball that many times," said Deion Branch, who was named the game's MVP after he caught 11 passes for 133 yards to tie the Super Bowl record.

RIGHT PLACE, RIGHT TIME

Could there possibly be any more doubts?

The best team in football has just concluded a grueling four-week exam period in which it faced three completely different challenges from three very good football teams. You can make a case — in fact, I'm going to — that this was the most difficult post-season task ever presented to a team attempting to win a Super Bowl.

The grades? A-plus, A-plus, and A-minus. The scores? 20-3, 41-27, and, finally, 24-21. Yup, for the third time in four years the Patriots have become the champions of the known football universe with a 3-point victory. But 3 or 30, it,doesn't matter. The idea is to score more points than the other guys, and no team this century has found the weekly formula to do just that better than the New England Patriots.

Think about it: The New England Patriots are the unquestioned Team of the Century.

They are now in the enviable position of being able to judge championships. The first was, obviously, sweet. The second was vindicating and harrowing. But this one demanded a level of overall excellence that should make everyone involved feel incredibly proud. For what the Patriots have done in defeating these three particular teams in four weeks is nothing short of awe-inspiring.

"Indianapolis, we all know what kind of a team they are," said Bill Belichick. "Pittsburgh was the best team in the AFC all year. Philadelphia went wire-to-wire all year. I can't think of three tougher teams in my ex-

perience in the postseason."

This was a Patriots season unlike any other. After getting off to a 6-0 start, the entire season was threatened by the devastation of the secondary, forcing Belichick and his defensive staff to start improvising with players and schemes that made them the talk of both the NFL and the world of football in general. The brain trust had to make do with a converted wide receiver, a converted linebacker, and assorted people from the waiver wire. They kept winning and they made it look easy.

It was not.

The secondary nightmare continued right through last night, when starting free safety Eugene Wilson injured his

arm while performing special teams duty in the second quarter. This vaulted rookie Dexter Reid, a fourth-round pick from North Carolina, into the lineup. Were there scary moments? Oh, yes. Greg Lewis beat him for a touchdown in the fourth period, but the only thing that mattered was that he wasn't beaten more. He was good enough to get the job done, and on this team, Getting The Job Done is the only criterion for maintaining employment.

Rodney Harrison picks off a pass in front of teammate Tedy Bruschi, who celebrates his fourth-quarter interception, left.

But it wasn't easy, and finding a way to compete with the personnel at hand may have been the toughest challenge of Belichick's coaching career.

"I can't say enough about these players," said Belichick. "These guys have worked so hard for the last six months. They just stepped up, kept working, kept fighting, and they did it again today."

This game was work. The Eagles came completely as advertised defensively, holding Tom Brady & Co. to one first down and no points in the first quarter. Brady looked curiously uncomfortable in the kind of Big Game that has made his reputation.

It didn't last, of course, because Tom Brady really is Mr. Cool, and it was only a matter of time before he and his mentor, Charlie Weis, found out what would and wouldn't work against an aggressive, speedy Philly defensive unit. With the typical Patriot lack of flamboyance, the offense calmly executed five excellent drives after falling behind, 7-0.

The first ended in frustration when Brady botched a handoff to Kevin Faulk and wound up fumbling the ball away after he had apparently recovered it. But three of the next four possessions resulted in marches of 37, 69, and 66 yards for touchdowns and the following drive culminated in a 22-yard field goal by Adam Vinatieri that provided the Patriots with the eventual margin of victory.

We are used to seeing Brady do whatever is necessary to win. He is now 9-0 in three playoff visits. But Philadelphia defensive coordinator Jim Johnson apparently needs to see just a little more before he becomes a true Brady admirer. "Brady is on his way to being one of the better quarterbacks," he noted.

Thanks, coach. We'll keep our eye on him.

David Givens has reason to strut after catching a second-quarter touchdown pass.

Third

Boston toasted the first pro football dynasty of the 21st century with a "rolling rally" that took the Super Bowl champions from Hynes Convention Center area to Staniford Street. More than one million fans came out to salute their heroes.

time is the charm

PATRIOTIC FERVOR

Dave Gott and Mike Cuthbertson, sporting shiny headgear, Ashmi Pansholi, flashing three fingers, and the Hickey and Daly boys from Malden have a message for Tom Brady and Deion Branch, "This doesn't get old."

2004 ROSTER

#	NAME	POS	HT	WT	AGE	YR	WHEN/HOW ACQUIRED	COLLEGE
4	Adam Vinatieri	K	6'0"	202	32	9	1996 Rookie free agent	South Dakota State
6	Rohan Davey	QB	6'2"	245	26	3	2002 Draft—4th Round	Lousiana State
8	Josh Miller	P	6'4"	225	34	9	2004 free agent (PIT)	Arizona
10	Kevin Kasper	WR	6'1"	202	27	4	2004 free agent (ARZ)	Iowa
12	Tom Brady	QB	6'4"	225	27	5	1999 Draft—6th Round	Michigan
13	Jim Miller	QB	6'2"	225	33	10	2004 free agent (TB)	Michigan State
21	Randall Gay	CB	5'11"	186	22	R	2004 Rookie free agent	Lousiana State
22	Asante Samuel	CB	5'10"	185	23	2	2003 Draft—4th Round	Central Florida
24	Ty Law	CB	5'11"	200	30	10	1995 Draft—1st Round	Michigan
26	Eugene Wilson	DB	5'10"	195	24	2	2003 Draft—2nd Round	Illinois
27	Rabih Abdullah	RB	6'0"	235	29	7	2004 free agent (CHI)	Lehigh
28	**Corey Dillon**	**RB**	**6'1"**	**225**	**30**	**8**	**2003 Trade (CIN)**	**Washington**
29	Earthwind Moreland	CB	5'10"	182	27	3	2004 free agent (CLE)	Georgia Southern
30	Je'Rod Cherry	DB	6'1"	210	31	9	2001 free agent (PHI)	California
31	Hank Poteat	CB	5'10"	192	27	4	2004 free agent (CAR)	Pittsburgh
33	**Kevin Faulk**	**RB**	**5'8"**	**202**	**28**	**6**	**1999 Draft—2nd Round**	**Lousiana State**
34	Cedric Cobbs	RB	6'0"	225	23	R	2004 Draft—4th Round	Arkansas
35	Patrick Pass	FB	5'10"	217	27	5	2000 Draft—7th Round	Georgia
37	Rodney Harrison	S	6'1"	220	32	11	2003 free agent (SD)	Western Illinois
42	Dexter Reid	S	5'11"	203	23	R	2004 Draft—4th Round	North Carolina
48	Tully Banta-Cain	LB	6'2"	250	24	2	2003 Draft—7th Round	California
49	Eric Alexander	LB	6'2"	240	22	R	2004 Rookie free agent	Lousiana State
50	Mike Vrabel	LB	6'4"	261	29	8	2001 free agent (PIT)	Ohio State
51	Don Davis	LB	6'1"	235	32	9	2003 free agent (STL)	Kansas
52	Ted Johnson	LB	6'4"	253	32	10	1995 Draft—2nd Round	Colorado
53	Larry Izzo	LB	5'10"	228	30	9	2001 free agent (MIA)	Rice
54	Tedy Bruschi	LB	6'1"	247	31	9	1996 Draft—3rd Round	Arizona
55	Willie McGinest	LB	6'5"	270	33	11	1994 Draft—1st Round	Southern California
58	Matt Chatham	LB	6'4"	250	27	5	2000 Rookie free agent	South Dakota
59	Rosevelt Colvin	LB	6'3"	250	27	6	2003 free agent (CHI)	Purdue
61	Stephen Neal	G	6'4"	305	28	3	2001 Rookie free agent	Cal State-Bakersfield
63	Joe Andruzzi	G	6'3"	312	29	8	2000 free agent (GB)	S. Connecticut State
64	Gene Mruczkowski	G/C	6'2"	305	23	2	2003 Rookie free agent	Purdue
66	Lonie Paxton	LS	6'2"	260	26	5	2003 free agent (STL)	Sacramento State
67	Dan Koppen	C	6'2"	296	25	2	2003 Draft—5th Round	Boston College
71	Russ Hochstein	G	6'4"	305	26	4	2002 Rookie free agent	Nebraska
72	**Matt Light**	**T**	**6'4"**	**305**	**27**	**4**	**2001 Draft—2nd Round**	**Purdue**
75	Vince Wilfork	DL	6'2"	325	24	R	2004 Draft—1st Round	Miami (Fla.)

#	NAME	POS	HT	WT	AGE	YR	WHEN/HOW ACQUIRED	COLLEGE
76	Brandon Gorin	T	6'6"	308	26	3	2003 Waivers	Purdue
80	Troy Brown	WR	5'10"	196	33	12	1993 Draft—8th Round	Marshall
81	Bethel Johnson	WR	5'11"	200	24	2	2003 Draft—2nd Round	Texas A&M
82	Daniel Graham	TE	6'3"	257	25	3	2002 Draft—1st Round	Colorado
83	Deion Branch	WR	5'9"	193	25	3	2002 Draft—2nd Round	Louisville
85	Jed Weaver	TE	6'4"	258	28	6	2004 free agent (DEN)	Oregon
86	David Patten	WR	5'10"	190	30	8	2001 free agent (CLE)	Western Carolina
87	**David Givens**	**WR**	**6'0"**	**215**	**24**	**3**	**2002 Draft—7th Round**	**Notre Dame**
88	Christian Fauria	TE	6'4"	250	33	10	2001 free agent (SEA)	Colorado
91	Marquise Hill	DE	6'6"	300	22	R	2004 Draft—2nd Round	Lousiana State
93	**Richard Seymour**	**DL**	**6'6"**	**310**	**25**	**4**	**2001 Draft—1st Round**	**Georgia**
94	Ty Warren	DL	6'5"	300	22	2	2003 Draft—1st Round	Texas A&M
95	Roman Phifer	LB	6'2"	248	36	14	2001 free agent (NYJ)	UCLA
97	Jarvis Green	DL	6'3"	290	25	3	2004 Draft—4th Round	Lousiana State
98	Keith Traylor	DT	6'2"	340	35	13	2004 free agent (CHI)	Central State (OK)
99	Ethan Kelley	DT	6'2"	310	24	1	2003 Draft—7th Round	Baylor

PRACTICE SQUAD

#	NAME	POS	HT	WT	AGE	YR	WHEN/HOW ACQUIRED	COLLEGE
18	Cedric James	WR	6'1"	197	25	1	2004 free agent	Texas Christian
19	Ricky Bryant	WR	6'0"	185	23	R	2004 free agent	Hofstra
23	Omare Lowe	DB	6'1"	195	26	1	2004 free agent	Washington
32	Kory Chapman	RB	6'1"	202	24	R	2004 free agent	Jacksonville State
47	Justin Kurpeikis	LB	6'3"	254	27	3	2004 free agent	Penn State
65	Lance Nimmo	T	6'5"	303	25	1	2004 free agent	West Virginia
69	Buck Rasmussen	DL	6'4"	285	25	1	2004 free agent	Nebraska-Omaha
75	Billy Yates	G	6'2"	305	24	1	2004 free agent	Texas A&M

COACHES

HEAD COACH Bill Belichick
ASSISTANTS: DEFENSIVE COORDINATOR Romeo Crennel / WIDE RECEIVERS Brian Daboll
RUNNING BACKS Ivan Fears / ASSISTANT OFFENSIVE LINE & TIGHT ENDS Jeff Davidson
DEFENSIVE LINE Pepper Johnson / DEFENSIVE BACKS Eric Mangini / QUARTERBACKS Josh McDaniels
COACHING ASSISTANT Matt Patricia / ASSISTANT STRENGTH & CONDITIONING Markus Paul /
LINEBACKERS Dean Pees / ASSISTANT HEAD COACH & OFFENSIVE LINE Dante Scarnecchia /
SPECIAL TEAMS Brad Seely / COACHING ASSISTANT Cory Undin
OFFENSIVE COORDINATOR Charlie Weis / STRENGTH & CONDITIONING Mike Woicik

2001

Ended season with 9 consecutive victories, including
stunning upset of the Rams in the Super Bowl.

POSTSEASON Tom Brady is a perfect 9-0 as the Patriots'

2003
Began their historic 21-game winning streak with victory over Tennessee on October 5.

2004
Super Bowl win over Eagles completed a 32-2 run since a 2-2 start to the '03 season.

starting quarterback during postseason play.